Tending to the Holy

Tending to the Holy

THE PRACTICE OF THE PRESENCE OF GOD IN MINISTRY

Bruce G. Epperly
and
Katherine Gould Epperly

THE
ALBAN
INSTITUTE
Herndon, Virginia
www.alban.org

The Alban Institute
2121 Cooperative Way, Suite 100
Herndon, VA 20171

Scripture quotations, unless otherwise noted, are from the New Revised Standard Version of the Bible, copyright © 1989, Division of Christian Education of the National Council of Churches of Christ in the United States of America, and are used by permission.

Scripture quotations noted as KJV are from The Holy Bible, King James Version.

Cover design by Signal Hill.

Library of Congress Cataloging-in-Publication Data

Epperly, Bruce Gordon.
   Tending to the holy : the practice of the presence of God in ministry / Bruce G. Epperly and Katherine Gould Epperly.
      p. cm.
   Includes bibliographical references (p. 187).
   ISBN 978-1-56699-391-3
   1. Spirituality. 2. Church work. 3. Pastoral theology. I. Epperly, Katherine Gould, 1950- II. Title.
   BV4501.3.E68 2009
   248.8'92--dc22
                              2009021026

      09   10   11   12   13   VP   5   4   3   2   1

Contents

FOREWORD

"Most of us are pretty eclectic anyway," the speaker said, touting the value of multiple theological and spiritual traditions. During a break, two of us shared our instant response, "No, not eclectic, but integrative!" Too much of what passes for "spirituality" presents us with a mishmash of ideas and practices from which to pick and choose bits and pieces in the hope that we can break the boredom of worship or a board meeting or personal burnout.

What ministers need and what hungry seekers yearn for is integrity: to walk the talk, to practice a life of contemplation that manifests love in action. We need a way of integrating ancient practices in a coherent fashion in every facet of personal and communal life. We long for genuine God moments not just in the overtly "spiritual" areas of preaching, teaching, worship, and pastoral care, but also in the grit of administration, finances, and leadership—often despite dysfunctional systems. And all this is for one purpose: to extend the radical hospitality of God—mirroring the life of Jesus in every level of personal, interpersonal, political, and global environments. What would it look like to practice the presence of God in ministry?

"Tending to the holy" is like tending a fire—fanning the sparks of authentic divine presence even in the most maddening individual or institutional conflicts. This book's title rings true to the integrity so deeply needed to develop organizational structures that exhibit the organic spiritual core of who we are:

agents of God's reconciling love in a broken world, ambassa-
dors of a peace that surpasses human understanding. To tend
the spark of divine love in the most narrow-minded church
member or in the crudest criminal is to practice the Quaker
principle of "answering to that of God in every human being."

"Days pass, years vanish, and we walk sightless among miracles," runs an old Hebrew prayer.[1] How can we sharpen our
eyes to tend the holy fires all around us? Three features leap out
on nearly every page of Bruce and Kate Epperly's book. First,
the authors constantly invite us to practice the presence of God
in the push and tug of real community, in contrast to much of
what today centers on "my" spirituality.

Second, many a solo author prescribes simplistic spiritual
practices that make you say, "These may work for that author,
but never with my personality type." Because Bruce and Kate
have very distinct personalities, what they offer us is not a one-
size-fits-all prescription but rather an invitation to a multicol-
ored tapestry for practicing the presence of God. For example,
introverted Bruce rises early to sit in silence and walk, while
extroverted Kate rises late to practice writing, art journaling,
and active conversations.

In my own years of teaching at Lancaster Theological Seminary, on many occasions I witnessed Bruce excusing himself
to practice a Celtic "encircling prayer," taking a walk around
the campus to clear his mind and pray for his students before
teaching an afternoon class. And Kate, during a workshop I
was leading where she was a participant, over lunch offered
spontaneously to lead the group in a watercoloring process of
prayer awareness. It was an ideal model of tapping the community's gifts—just what I had been advocating based on my book
*The Soul of Tomorrow's Church: Weaving Spiritual Practices in
Ministry Together*.[2]

Third, the threads that hold this tapestry together are the
real-life stories woven into page after page as you read. Here
is incarnational spirituality. No sooner do you read about an

insightful idea than the authors give a story: you visualize the thing actually happening in the life of a minister or a suffering congregant, in a board meeting or a worship experience. Stories are the art medium by which the Word becomes flesh (see John 1:14). Clarissa Pinkola Estés says:

> I hope you will go out and let stories happen to you, and that you will work with them, water them with your blood and tears and your laughter till they bloom, till you yourself burst into bloom. Then you will see what medicines they make, and where and when to apply them. That is the work. The only work.[3]

In a high-tech world, Kate and Bruce Epperly are passionate about rejuvenating so-called mainline churches. Their paradigm consists of raising honest questions and recounting stories of transformation that create a passion for sharing the Good News: these are the two primary methods of the Master Teacher Jesus and teachers in all spiritual traditions.

How can one develop genuine faith, faith that is passionate *and* open to question itself, willing to shed its outgrown shell for a new creature to be born? A friend challenged me: "What gives you such a passion to communicate if you (a minister!) don't think people are going to hell if they're not in a 'church'"? We came up with two reasons: rigid exclusiveness creates a hell on earth, and individualist love without community is powerless to create a loving person or peaceful world.

So how can you avoid these twin roads to hell on earth: clutching rigid beliefs with a "crusade" mentality or falling for anything-goes individualism? Here is the foundation thread woven throughout this book: by following your soul's path with some fellow pilgrims, rather than alone, you become a more loving and genuine person and more aware of moments of healing beauty right in the world's brokenness.

Somewhere between wallowing in spiritual apathy and fleeing to dangerous religion we catch a clue. *Tending to the Holy* invites you to begin looking for traces of grace right here, right now—in the ordinary stuff of suffering and surprise—then to share the stories.

GRIT SEASONING*

While I do this grit
work, season
the irksome pieces
with enough
Ahas! to remind me
of the reason.

—Kent Ira Groff

Rev. Dr. Kent Ira Groff
Author, *Active Spirituality: A Guide for Seekers and Ministers*

Copyright © 2009 by Kent Ira Groff

ACKNOWLEDGMENTS

A Word of Thanksgiving

If the only prayer you can say is "Thank you," that will be enough. These words, attributed to the German mystic Meister Eckhart, serve as the inspiration for the final text of our trilogy on pastoral spirituality. The two of us are grateful to the many pastors who have been part of Lancaster Theological Seminary's programs in pastoral excellence and spiritual formation. These pastors have sought to be faithful to their vocation as spiritual leaders amid the complexities and uncertainties of the twenty-first century. Their fidelity to God, their congregations, and to their spouses, partners, and families have inspired our work. We have been blessed to have heard and now share stories of faithful and challenging ministerial leadership, and though most of these pastors remain anonymous in this text, we have been honored to be part of their holy adventure.

We are also abundantly grateful to Bruce's colleagues at Lancaster Theological Seminary, most especially President Riess Potterveld and Dean Edwin David Aponte and the Office of Continuing Education staff, Kathy Harvey Nelson, April Anderson, Rikki Jones, and David Mellott. We are grateful to the faithful community of Christians at Disciples United Community Church in Lancaster, Pennsylvania, with whom we seek to proclaim God's inclusive hospitality and share solid theological reflection. We continue to be grateful to the Lilly Endowment, under the direction of Craig Dykstra and John Wimmer, whose generosity has made possible our work with pastors in every season of ministry. We are also grateful to Richard Bass, publishing director at the Alban Institute, and his expert staff, including Andrea Lee. We give thanks for Diane Hetherington's friendship as well as her wisdom about appreciative inquiry and reflection.

We gratefully remember our own teachers and mentors in ministry and theological reflection whose faithfulness to God and extraordinary theological insight have transformed both students and congregations and inspired a generation of dedicated spiritual leaders and seminary, college, and seminary professors. Without their inspiration this trilogy would never have been written. We especially honor John Akers, Howard Clinebell, John B. Cobb Jr., George L. "Shorty" Collins, Clayton Gooden, David Griffin, Allan Armstrong Hunter, and Bernard Loomer. Bruce is ever grateful to his father, Everett Epperly, whose love of God and commitment to faithful ministry first inspired him to study theology and explore the ministry. In the spirit of those who have inspired us, we dedicate this book to pastors everywhere who seek to join faithful ministry with healthy relationships and abundant living.

Epiphany 2009

Practicing the Presence of God in Ministry

When Emily first experienced the call to ordained ministry, her whole world was transformed. Deep in her heart, she experienced the gentle movements of God's spirit that brought gladness and peace to everyday life. Her perspective on life completely changed as she experienced ordinary encounters as opportunities to experience God's presence and to share the good news that "Christ is alive!" In seminary, Emily's sense of call to ordained ministry matured as she wrestled with new images of God in her theology classes and grew in her ministerial skills and vocational identity under the direction of a wise field-education supervisor, who reminded her that even on the busiest pastoral days, she needed to take time for prayerful contemplation. "If you don't see Christ in your study while you're preparing your sermon or in the hospital room when you're visiting a parishioner following surgery, how will you be able to share God's love with people who come to you with all their pain and doubt?" she counseled Emily. Her field education mentor reminded her that pastors are called to be visionaries whose vocation is to "seek Christ's presence in everyone they encounter, including themselves."

Now in her tenth year of ministry and leading a growing suburban congregation, Emily is trying to reclaim the lively experience of God that accompanied her initial sense of call to ordained ministry. Recently, Emily noticed that her pastoral day had become more of a task than a blessing as she went from meeting to meeting and appointment to appointment. Emily admitted that "in order to respond to the details of successful congregational ministry, I had placed my spiritual life in the background, and now I was paying the price for my haphazard, 'drive-by' approach to prayer and study. If I'm to remain a spiritually centered and vital pastor, able share the good news of God's grace with my congregation, I need to make a real commitment to renewing my ministry through prayer, meditation, study, and sabbath keeping."

With the support of her spiritual director, Emily made a commitment to begin practicing the presence of God in ministry by more intentionally setting aside a period of time each day for prayer and devotional reading. Knowing how easy it is to let the daily tasks of ministry take precedence over her prayer life, she now blocks off in advance an hour each day for prayer and devotional reading with the same intentionality that she sets aside time for sermon preparation, congregational administration, and pastoral care. Emily announced to her staff and congregational lay leadership that, apart from a congregational emergency, these times of prayer and reflection would be nonnegotiable elements of her ministry. While Emily still struggles with taking time for prayer and devotional reading and seldom gets a full day for sabbath, she recognizes that the quality of her pastoral care, administration, spiritual counsel, worship leadership, and preaching has improved and that she feels less fragmented by the many demands of her ministry.

Also, as a result of her renewed commitment to prayer and self-care, Emily is regaining her pastoral vision. She is more present to what is going on in herself and the lives of her parishioners, and she is more open to experiencing God in the everyday encounters and responsibilities of family life and congregational ministry. Emily prepares herself to respond creatively and calmly to the unexpected and chaotic moments of ministry by taking time for quiet contemplation on a regular basis.

As you reflect on Emily's story in light of your current experience in ministry, does her experience sound familiar? Is your ministry still fresh, lively, and growing? Are you experiencing God's call to explore new ways of integrating your spiritual leadership and pastoral care? Is your prophetic voice haranguing or reconciling in the ears of those with whom you theologically and politically disagree? Do you wish you could regain the spiritual sensitivity that once accompanied your pastoral vision?

The past several years of working with pastors in every season of ministry have convinced the two of us that lively, effective, and spiritually centered ministry is the result of a pastor's ongoing commitment to deepen her or his experience of God through intentionally practicing the presence of God throughout the many responsibilities of ministry. While we believe that God inspires pastors and laypeople in every moment and every encounter, we also believe that a pastor's ability to experience and share God's guiding, sustaining, and inspiring presence is related to the quality of her or his spiritual life. Practicing the presence of God in ministry is a lively partnership that must be nurtured and developed like any other intimate relationship. As spiritual leaders of their congregations, pastors are, first and foremost, called to tend the holy in their own lives.

Our mutual concern for supporting pastoral spiritual growth amid the concrete and often challenging tasks of ministry inspired us to write this book. For the past several years, Bruce has directed Lancaster (PA) Theological Seminary's pastoral excellence and spiritual formation groups for ordained ministers in every season of ministry, from first congregational call to retirement. Kate has been mentor and spiritual guide to numerous seminarians and pastors in her roles of pastoral counselor, spiritual director, and field education supervisor. We have observed that pastors can flourish in every aspect of their ministry and respond creatively to the challenges of congregational life when they place regular commitments to prayer and contemplation, along with continuing theological and professional education, at the center their many pastoral activities. Our work together in leading colleague groups in Lancaster Theological Seminary's Wholeness in Ministry program for newly ordained pastors, who are making the transition from seminary to their first congregational call, has given us the opportunity to support newly ordained ministers in their quest to be faithful, skilled, effective, and spiritually centered pastors in the midst of demanding ministerial schedules and the rapidly changing cultural dislocation of the postmodern world. In our work with these new pastors as well as pastors in every season of ministry, we seek to help them discover ways to maintain and heighten their vision of Christ's lively presence in the many roles of ministry and family life.

Our goal in this book is to share insights from our own and other pastors' spiritual adventures as we have sought to experience God in the everyday, repetitive tasks of ministry.[1] We hope to join theological reflection, spiritual formation, and concrete ministerial guidance in ways that will serve as catalysts for your own practice of God's presence in ministry.

Transforming Practices

Today there is a growing interest in reclaiming and reforming the ancient practices of Christian faith as sources of inspiration for vital twenty-first century Christianity. Diana Butler Bass asserts that commitment to life-transforming Christian practices, such as healing, prayer, service, and hospitality, is essential to the renewal of mainstream Christianity.[2] She suggests that living out these practices in daily life nurtures a uniquely Christian way of life and vision of reality that enables laypeople and pastors alike to experience the world through the eyes of faith. According to Dorothy Bass and Craig Dykstra, "practices are things Christian people do together in response to and in light of God's active presence in the life of the world."[3] Inspired by an affirmation of God's graceful and creative presence in the ordinary details of life, spiritual practices enable us to *experience* what we believe and *live* by what we experience by affirming the seamless fabric of God's presence in all things.

The wise counsel of innovative congregational and ministerial guides such as Diana Butler Bass, Dorothy Bass, and Craig Dykstra, evident in their quest to reclaim traditional faith practices in light of the unique challenges of the postmodern age, calls us to reclaim the wisdom of our "parents" in the spiritual journey as foundational for our pastoral practices today.

Foremost among our parents in practicing the presence of God is Brother Lawrence, a seventeenth-century Carmelite layperson, who penned the spiritual classic, *The Practice of the Presence of God*. This humble "kitchen mystic" saw all of life as a response to God's ever-present and loving presence. According to Brother Lawrence, "the most holy and necessary practice in the Christian life is the presence of God."[4] Whether in the kitchen, running an errand, buying provisions, or receiving the Eucharist, Brother Lawrence asserted that our calling as Christians is simply to be attentive to God's presence in our lives. Following the apostle Paul's counsel to "pray without ceasing" (1 Thess. 5:17), Brother Lawrence advised that "whatever we do, even if we are reading the Word or praying, we should stop for a few minutes—as often as possible—to praise God, to enjoy [God] there in secret."[5]

A century later, Jesuit spiritual guide Jean-Pierre de Caussade described a similar spiritual journey in terms of the "sacrament of the present moment." According to de Caussade, God speaks to us in every moment and each encounter. The spiritual life is grounded in the "immediate communication with God" by which we recognize that each moment brings "its appointed task, faithfully to be accomplished."[6] Our task as followers of Jesus is simply to follow "the will of God in whatever form it might present itself."[7]

Both men embodied the Benedictine wisdom of seeing and responding to Christ in every guest and encounter. As spiritual guide and Benedictine lay member Norvene Vest notes in her contemporary commentary on the Rule of St. Benedict, a classic in monastic spirituality penned by Benedict of Nursia (480–547 CE), "the whole orientation of the Rule is to the principle that God is everywhere, all the time, and thus that every element of our ordinary day is potentially holy."[8] Like all Benedictines, Norvene Vest suggests that our attentiveness to God, even in the smallest details of daily life, transforms our world from a series of unrelated events to a unified, albeit open-ended, holy adventure in which God guides and inspires us in every encounter. In the current culture, busy pastors ask whether or not the spirit that gave birth to monasteries as places of daily spiritual mindfulness and devotion can be experienced today as they struggle to view the complexities of everyday life through the eyes of Christ.

As we seek to practice God's presence in our ministerial lives, we pastors must admit that our lives are not simple or cloistered like those of our spiritual parents. Today, many faithful, but overcommitted, pastors identify with Jacob's dream of a "ladder of angels." After awakening from a vivid dream in which Jacob visualizes angels ascending to heaven and then descending again, Jacob exclaims "Surely the LORD is in this place—and I did not know it! . . . How awesome is this place! This is none other than the house of God, and this is the gate of heaven" (Gen. 28:16–17). Amid the many tasks of ministry and the hectic schedules that blind us to the deeper spiritual realities of personal and professional lives, our calling is to pause and, then, notice that God is with us in what author Kathleen Norris describes as the "quotidian mysteries"—the everyday moments of holiness with which the everyday lives of pastors and their parishioners are filled: the face of a preschool child; the wisdom of a woman who recounts her eight decades of congregational commitment; the holy struggle of an adolescent honestly sharing questions about his sexual identity; a college student awakening to her life's vocation; or a busy parent experiencing at midlife the call to a deeper spiritual life, and possibly seminary. While God's graceful vision may come upon us by surprise and without any intentionality on our part, we may also encounter God's wisdom as a result of intentionally committing ourselves to holistic spiritual practices that open us to the presence of God in our daily ministerial tasks. While our spiritual practices do not *create* God's graceful presence in our lives, they can enable us to experience and intensify our awareness of God's grace and inspiration within our pastoral encounters in such a way that we can come to affirm amid the details of pastoral ministry, "Surely God is in this place—we know it" not only intellectually, but spiritually, physically, and relationally.

The two of us have faced for many years the multilayered spiritual challenges that characterize our lives as members of the "sandwich generation": we continue to care for Kate's ninety-one-year-old mother, who lives with us, and Bruce's fifty-nine-year-old mentally disabled brother, who lives nearby, and have supported, over the past year, our son and his wife as our son faced a life-threatening illness during their first year of marriage. All the while we have sought to be faithful to our many professional callings: pastoral ministry, academic administration, and seminary teaching. As a result of our own experiences as pastors, we know how easy it is for the good and growing seed of faithful ministry, first experienced in our call to follow Jesus into ordained ministry, to be choked and stunted by the weeds of personal and professional busyness. Still, we believe that every pastor's life can bring forth a "harvest of righteousness" as a result of cultivating spiritual practices that define and transform their lives (Phil. 1:11). We describe pathways to experiencing spiritual vitality and effectiveness in the first two books of our trilogy on ministerial spirituality, *Feed the Fire: Avoiding Clergy Burnout* and *Four Seasons of Ministry: Gathering a Harvest of Righteousness*.[9]

In the next few paragraphs, we will share practices that have defined our own spiritual journeys and shaped our respective bivocational ministries. While we recognize our own unique path as clergy couple, one of whom has joined congregational and university ministry with seminary teaching, ministerial mentoring, and academic administration, and the other of whom has joined congregational ministry with pastoral counseling and spiritual direction, we believe that our stories can serve as an inspiration for other pastors in their quest to practice the presence of God in their ministries. Bruce's daily spiritual practices reflect his personality type (INFJ) and his innately disciplined and consistent approach to life.[10] Each morning Bruce rises before sunrise with the affirmation from the Psalms, "This is the day that God has made and I will rejoice and be glad in it." As he shuffles around the house, brushing his teeth, feeding the cats, and, in wintertime, lighting the morning fire, he prepares for each day by pondering the question, "What great thing will happen in my life today?" Each morning, he practices a form of centering prayer, which he learned nearly forty years ago as a first-year college student. This centering practice involves graceful focus on a particular prayer word as a means of deepening his experience of God in the present moment and the day to come. Following his prayer time, Bruce takes a two- to four-mile walk, devoting part of his morning walk to repeating spiritual affirmations, prayers of petition and intercession, and opening to divine energy filling and enlivening his body, mind, spirit, and relationships. He almost always returns home refreshed and ready to study or write for an hour or so before Kate rises to greet the day.

In recent years, Kate, an ENFP, has added the practice of knitting to her lifetime of journaling as part of her daily prayers.[11] As a participant in her congregation's prayer shawl ministry, Kate experiences contemplative knitting as a way to focus her mind and pray for the persons for whom she and the prayer shawl group have a special care, in addition to the particular person who will receive the shawl she is knitting. As someone who does not like repetition or rigid schedules, the practice of journaling enables Kate to take measure of the time she is dedicating to prayer amid the challenges she faces in her quest to be a faithful pastor, spouse, mother, and daughter. In the course of her work day, Kate often gives a simple "Alleluia" chant as she does housekeeping chores, works on worship services, or drives to pastoral calls. Her favorite prayer time, however, is on-her-knees "sweat prayers" while working in the garden or walking with colleagues in ministry. Her more activist approach to practicing God's presence reflects her more extraverted temperament and preference for spontaneity.

We both prayerfully savor our first cup of coffee each morning. In the spirit of Joyce Rupp's *The Cup of Our Life*, the two of us see the first cup of coffee as much more than a caffeine jolt to begin the day, but a ritual of embracing the day to come that joins the "relaxation response" of repetitive spiritual activity with the holy sensuousness of taste and smell.[12]

We both have learned to anchor our busy and often complex daily schedules in mindfulness of our breathing, grounded in awareness of God's ever-present spirit. As one who shifts gears from professor, writer, pastor, spiritual guide, and administrator on an hourly basis throughout the day, Bruce, in particular, has learned the importance of pausing to take a breath as a means of spiritual centering and weaving together the many activities of his day into a tapestry of spiritual transformation. As he moves from one task to another or answers the phone or a knock on his seminary study door, Bruce takes a moment to close his eyes and take a few gentle breaths of opening and centering. These few breaths enable him to encounter the next task of the day with grace, calm, and clarity. As a result of our commitment to breathing in God's spirit as we go from task to task, the two of us have come to realize that in the varied movements of the day, we are really doing only *one thing*, and that is responding to God's graceful and enlightening presence in each moment's experience.

As you reflect on our approaches as working pastors to practicing God's presence in our lives and ministry, we invite you to take a few moments now to consider the spiritual practices that sustain and transform your ministry and enable you to maintain your pastoral vision. You may find that you have more "spiritual practices" than you might initially imagine, especially if you include activities as simple and repetitive as drinking a cup of coffee or prayerful breathing. What spiritual practices center and inspire you in the course of the everyday activities of your professional life? How might you give them a deeper spiritual intention? As you ponder these questions, remember that effective practices of opening to God's presence will always reflect your personality type, theological perspective, and professional and personal context.

Although Christianity has a long and holy tradition of spiritual practices, we want to remind you that there is no *one* appropriate way to practice God's presence in your life and ministry. We Christians are free to explore a wide variety of holistic spiritual practices that emerge from and nurture God's unique, yet contextual and embodied, presence in our lives. In the spirit of Jesus's ministry, we can go to a lonely place to pray or find wholeness in healthy companionship with our congregants and professional colleagues.

Practicing Theological and Spiritual Transformation

To be sure, practicing the presence of God in ministry must be grounded in solid theological reflection and in a commitment to explore both traditional and innovative spiritual practices. Our worldview and theology profoundly shape our sense of the presence and activity of God. The integration of theological reflection and spiritual practice is especially important for those pastoral leaders and teachers who are called to share God's presence with their congregations. We must be both teachers and witnesses to the lively and transforming faith we affirm. The two of us are convinced that a pastor's theological vision shapes, in large measure, the spiritual practices that inform her or his life and ministry. While we recognize a good deal of truth in the postmodern critique of any attempt to frame global and all-inclusive theological worldviews, we nevertheless affirm the value of articulating a coherent, yet tentative and flexible, theological vision of God's activity in the world as a means of orienting our lives and daily spiritual practices.

Our own ministerial vision of reality has been influenced greatly by process theology, ancient and contemporary Christian mystical traditions, insights from contemporary physics and cosmology, Jungian psychology, and the practical wisdom of family and congregational systems theory. Our spiritual practices both reflect and shape our evolving theological vision.

As you reflect on the theological vision that shapes your spiritual practices, the two of us invite you to consider the relationship between three primary and interdependent dimensions of personal and professional life: (1) your theological perspective and understanding of prayer, (2) the role your body plays in spiritual formation, and (3) the interplay between action and contemplation in your life of faith and pastoral ministry. Does your vision of God support your spiritual practices and ministerial commitments? Where do practices of self-care and physical well-being fit into your understanding of God's presence in your life and ministry? In what ways do your spiritual practices inspire and sustain your commitment to social transformation?

In the following paragraphs, we will share the theological and spiritual affirmations that inspire and unite our own experiences of God's presence in the daily dynamics of ministry, marriage, parenting, teaching, administration, mentoring, and family and community life as a way of inspiring your own creative and personal theological reflection and intuitive discernment, no matter what your personality type or theological orientation. Our practices of the presence of God in our ministries are inspired by the following theological affirmations:

First, *God is present in every moment of our experience, in-cluding every personal and professional encounter.* As the apostle Paul proclaims, God is the lively and intimate reality "in whom we live and move and have our being" (Acts 17:28). We be-lieve that each moment of experience emerges as a result of God's inspiration, nurture, and energy. Because God is present in all things and all experiences, we can experience God's guid-ance and inspiration in the daily tasks of ministry, family life, and personal self-care with equal vitality and power. Spiritual practices enable us to bring to conscious awareness the Spirit's "sighs too deep for words" (Rom. 8:26) that give both guidance and comfort.

Second, *the Spirit present in every encounter and experi-ence is the source of possibility and transformation.* God, as the scripture says, is constantly doing a "new thing" (Isa. 43:19). Though constantly sustaining people through all the seasons of life, God's faithfulness is also "new every morning" (Jer. 3:23). Indeed, God's fidelity stems precisely from God's ability to re-spond with new and creative options for every situation in life and ministry. Faithfulness to God involves openness not only to new experiences but also to new practices and approaches to God's presence in people's lives. The Protestant affirmation "the reformation is constantly reforming" refers equally to spiritual practices, approaches to congregational leadership, and under-standing of God's activity. God is still speaking in our world and in our lives, and yet few of us adequately trust in divine novelty and surprise, or rehearse our memories of divine fidel-ity and steadfast love. What does it really mean to live by a belief in God's ever-present steadfast love and constant creativ-ity? At the very least, the two of us believe that it means we are called to vital, fresh, and novel forms of ministry, spiritual practice, and congregational life.

Third, *the ever-present and dynamic God seeks abundant life in all things.* Jesus revealed God's intention for the world and our lives with the words, "I came that they might have life, and have it abundantly" (John 10:10). Accordingly, we pursue spiritual practices that call us to embrace life in all its fullness rather than diminishing the beauty and wonder of life. God seeks wholeness in body, mind, spirit, and relationships and gives us more than we can ever imagine in support of our quest to join faithful ministry with responsive relationships.

Fourth, *the God who seeks abundant life also invites us to live an integrated life that includes wholeness of mind, body, spirit, and relationships.* God's lively, creative, and all-encompassing presence promotes a spirituality of wholeness that embraces every aspect of our lives. Prayer and contemplation are not just "spiritual" in the traditional sense of the word but are also "embodied" in our diet, exercise, and social concern. Healthy spiritual practices move us toward integrating rather than compartmentalizing the many spheres of our lives. They involve personal unity of body-mind-spirit as well as integrity in our relationships, beginning with family life and personal self-care.

Fifth, *God's presence and inspiration are both personal and global in nature.* Healthy spiritual practices nurture our personal lives as well as awaken us to ecological awareness and care for creation. Spirituality embraces the prophetic quest for justice and reconciliation for humans and nonhumans alike. As the biblical tradition attests, God calls to us through the lilies of the field, the birds of the air, and the creatures of land and sea. With every prayerful breath, we join creation's prayer for wholeness. Holistic spirituality lives by the psalmist's affirmation, "Let everything that breathes praise [God]" (Ps. 150:6).

Sixth, *God's presence in the world promotes creativity and freedom in our personal and professional lives.* Practicing the presence of God awakens us to a world in which the future is open and our actions truly make a difference. In contrast to those who believe that past, present, and future in their entirety have already been determined by God, we assert that spiritual formation calls us to be innovative creators and artists in partnership with a creative and innovative God. Like a good parent,

God encourages the creativity and freedom of God's beloved children. While our momentary actions may appear to have little impact, faithful and prayerful actions performed by people and communities over a lifetime can transform lives and communities and become tipping points in the quest for abundant life for ourselves and the planet as a whole.[13]

Ordinary Miracles

Kathleen Norris notes that "human love is sanctified not in the height of attraction and enthusiasm but in the everyday struggles of living with another person. It is not in romance but in routine that the possibilities for transformation are made manifest. And that requires commitment."[14] Maintaining a pastoral vision of Christ's presence is the result of day-to-day commitments to live intentionally as well as innovatively through holistic spiritual practices and acts of loving inclusion. This "miracle of mindfulness," described by Vietnamese Buddhist monk Thich Nhat Hanh, is found in our willingness to pause and open to God's oft-hidden presence in the mundane tasks of ministry and domestic life.[15]

The ordinary miracles of ministry are found everywhere for those who nurture an intentional and spiritually grounded pastoral vision. Practicing awareness of God's presence keeps our ministries fresh, vital, and inspiring for others and ourselves. Even the most challenging ministerial days and most difficult pastoral encounters can reflect the light of God that shines through all things (John 1:5, 9). Even when a pastor must be assertive and self-differentiating with her congregation in difficult situations, a disciplined mindfulness of God's nearness can enable her to radiate a sense of peace when others might panic or succumb to anxiety-based problem solving. Cultivating God's presence in ministry can enable us to experience the peace that passes all understanding and discover new possibilities for responding to the challenges of congregational life and pastoral relationships.

Practicing the Presence of God in Ministry

Each chapter concludes with a spiritual practice intended to awaken your experience of God's presence in the everyday tasks of ministry. These practices are reminders that you can tend to God's presence in your life in a variety of ways. It is clear to the two of us as individuals with two very different personalities, however, that there are no "one size fits all" spiritual practices. Accordingly, please feel free to adapt each practice to your personality and lifestyle. Drawn to the apostle Paul's image of the Spirit's "sighs too deep for words" constantly interceding on our behalf, we believe that God is present in all things as the source of life, possibility, and energy. God's desire for wholeness and transformation is, as we have previously noted, both universal and personal, and when trusted can sustain us for the long haul.

An intentionally God-aware and self-aware ministry reflects the dynamic and varied movements of one and the same reality. Pastors can experience God's unique desire for their lives and ministries in the many regular acts of ministry: as they prepare sermons in their studies, meet parishioners for coffee, bring order to the chaos of wedding rehearsals, or give guidance in a congregational board meeting. When we open to practicing the presence of God in ministry with a high level of intentionality, we open to the holiness and wonder of everything else in our personal and professional lives.

As we begin with you the journey of practicing the presence of God in ministry, we would like to share a process of God-awareness and self-awareness that has shaped our own personal and professional lives. Creatively adapted from the work of psychiatrist, author, and spiritual guide Gerald May, this process of awareness involves the following five steps: *pausing, noticing, opening, yielding and stretching,* and *responding.* Like the breath prayer Bruce practices as a form of God-awareness interspersed between professional tasks, our adaptation of Gerald May's approach can be employed both as a momentary call to awareness, consecrating our ministries, or as a regular practice of self-examination.[16] May notes that "authentic spiritual practice is nothing other than consecration in action. It is feeling your deepest desire, claiming it as a freshly born hope, offering it to God, and consciously living it as fully as you can."[17] According to May, this approach to self-awareness can be playfully described in terms of someone calling to us, "Hey, wake up! Here you are! Look! Taste! See! Appreciate!"[18] We describe the following process in terms of call and response, and gratitude and transformation. All the other spiritual practices of consecrating the tasks of ministry emerge from this simple practice.

First, take a moment to *pause* amid the busyness of your ministerial day. Pastors can create rituals of pausing by just taking a few deep breaths, turning off the computer, going for a brief walk, splashing water on your face, or moving from the desk chair to an easy chair. The pause that transforms is as simple as the psalmist's counsel to "be still, and know" that God is in and with us (Ps. 46:10).

Second, *notice* and become aware of how you feel at this very moment. This very moment, to paraphrase the psalmist, is the moment God has made! Take a moment to scan your body from head to toe. Notice how your body feels, the quality of your breath and your overall sense of well-being. Once you are present to yourself, take a moment to notice your emotional life. Are you feeling calm, hurried, anxious, rested, or fatigued? Notice your environment—the chirping of birds, the tick of the clock, the whirl of activity going on throughout the church building, the voices of preschool children.

Third, as your awareness of yourself and your environment deepens, *open* to the "sighs too deep for words," or what Gerald May calls "your most basic desire of the moment."[19] What is God's wisdom for you in the here and now? What yearnings move your spirit toward personal wholeness and service to others and to the planet? Let your experience of openness include offering your deepest desire of the moment to God, with the awareness that when you truly discover your deepest desires, you will discover God's desire and vision for your life. In so doing, you will experience your life as your most precious gift to God. With May, the two of us see this as a process of consecration by which you make sacred this holy moment and all the holy moments of your life by placing your desire in God's hands in the spirit of "thy will be done" or by opening your desires to the mysteries of God's abundance working through your desires to give you more than you can imagine in life.

Fourth, *yield and stretch* by choosing to listen for God's vision in your desires and, then, allowing God's vision to enlarge and stretch your vision of what is best for your family, congregation, and yourself. Let your stretching be a "reaching out" to claim God's gift of abundance for your congregation and yourself. Let your self-awareness in this holy moment connect you with God's presence moving through your life and the world.

Finally, in this process of *call and response*, as you stretch and reach out, let your intention be a commitment to embody more fully the vision of life and ministry you have received. Realistically, you may not fully or consciously know God's fresh vision for your life, and so you may simply ask God to lead, guide, and inspire you throughout the day.

In the spirit of Brother Lawrence, busy pastors can experience God's presence in every personal and professional situation. As a result of our prayerful intentionality, the ordinary and repetitive tasks of ministerial life—preaching and worship, spiritual formation, pastoral care, administration, and justice seeking—can deepen our spiritual lives and energize our ministries.

Wonder, Love, and Praise

PREACHING, TEACHING, AND WORSHIP
AS SPIRITUAL FORMATION

Reverend John Ames, the protagonist of Marilynne Robinson's *Gilead*, summarizes a lifetime of preaching with the following description of the preacher's life: "When you do this sort of work, it seems to be Sunday all the time, or Saturday night. You just finish preparing for one week, and it's already the next week."[1] This same sentiment was echoed by Kathy Harvey Nelson, associate director of continuing education at Lancaster Theological Seminary, a United Methodist pastor, with whom Bruce coleads ministerial excellence and spiritual formation groups for new pastors, "A preacher lives from Sunday to Sunday. You never really finish or have time to savor your success. As soon as I finish one sermon, I have to begin thinking about the next." A more cynical approach to preaching comes from a seasoned Disciples of Christ pastor, "You know, week after week, I feel that I must prove myself over and over again. In a consumer society, after all, you're only as good as your last sermon!"

For most pastors, the interplay of preaching, teaching, and worship leadership is at the heart of their public ministry. Congregational worship is the one opportunity pastors regularly have to nurture their parishioners' theological and spiritual growth. A pastor's leadership of worship, teaching, and preaching is the primary public vehicle not only for spiritual formation and theological reflection within her faith community but also for congregational outreach to the larger community.

Over the course of a ministerial career, nearly every pastor has to endure the threadbare joke, "It must be a great life, pastor, only working one hour a week!" As uncomfortable as that joke may be, especially to new pastors, it points out the historical significance of preaching and worship as the primary public means of inspiration, spiritual formation, and growth within Christian communities.

Despite preaching's importance in the public life of congregational ministers, we have found that many pastors are ambivalent about the role of preaching, teaching, and worship leadership in the church's life and in their own spiritual formation. Increasing weekday demands leave little time for preparation in these areas. Many pastors look longingly at the portrait of a pastor's life in the film *A River Runs Through It*—ample time for study of the classics and the Scriptures in the original languages, theological reflection, careful preparation, and regular opportunities for inspirational fly-fishing!

Mike Graves, professor of homiletics and worship at Central Baptist Theological Seminary in Shawnee, Kansas, raises the following question related to the pastor's vocation: "If preaching is intended to enliven the church, why is it killing so many pastors?" Graves notes that many pastors are experiencing, or close to experiencing, "homiletical burnout."[2] The rigors of weekly preaching seem to deaden, rather than enliven, many pastors' spiritual lives.

In this chapter, the two of us seek to respond to the challenge of homiletical and liturgical burnout by exploring ways in which we can practice the presence of God in the public acts of ministry—preaching, teaching, and worship leadership. We recognize the importance of preaching, teaching, and worship in transforming pastors and their congregations. Christian theologians, especially within the Reformed tradition, see word and sacrament as God's chosen vehicles for sharing the grace of God. Pastors in the evangelical and Wesleyan tradition see preaching as a call to decision, and progressive preachers see the act of preaching as aimed both at healing the planet and transforming our understanding of God and human existence. Holistically practicing the presence of God in preaching, teaching, and worship enables pastors to experience the graceful, healing, and transforming faith they affirm in their sermons.

In one way or another, virtually all pastors see the aim of preaching, worship leadership, and teaching as proclaiming the good news that awakens people to God's grace and inspires Christian spirituality and character formation in the midst of everyday life. The two of us believe that vital, life-transforming, and effective preaching, teaching, and worship leadership over the long haul must ultimately be grounded in the pastor's intimate experience of God's good news and graceful presence throughout her or his ministerial leadership. The life-transforming power of these public acts of ministry involves a lively interplay of prayerful contemplation and public witness, which nurture both the pastor and her or his community.

Our years of working with pastors in every season of ministry from first congregational call to retirement have led us to believe that most ordained ministers faithfully seek excellence in their preaching and worship leadership, but achieve it with increasing frustration and fatigue. Many pastors lament their inability to embody the rabbinical and spiritual leadership they imagined when they first experienced the call to ministry or as they prepared for their roles as teachers and preachers in seminary. As one newly ordained United Church of Christ pastor confessed, "I want to go deeper in my sermon preparation and liturgical studies. But, with the constant demands of building management, pastoral care, and conflict resolution, I don't have a lot of time to study or learn about other worship styles. I want to have time to do something well in ministry, but I feel like I'm failing." Another recently ordained Presbyterian pastor describes his guilt at "constantly failing to embody the scholarly care that I was taught in seminary." Their confessions are a wake-up call for pastors to explore the theological and spiritual dimensions of ministerial preaching, teaching, and worship leadership. Accordingly, in this chapter, we will suggest (1) a theology of revelation that helps enliven a pastor's public ministry and sharing the good news, (2) practices of spiritual formation and practical guidance for spiritual growth through preaching, worship, and teaching, and (3) practical ways that will enable pastors to experience excellence in their rabbinical and worship leadership.

Revealing the Gospel

Charles Wesley, hymn writer and leading figure in the Methodist movement, describes the experience of God in the ordinary and extraordinary moments of life in terms of "wonder, love, and praise."[3] Charles and his brother John experienced a lively sense of grace as the center of the Christian life. Although they were intimately aware of the brokenness of life, evident in their own personal struggles and in their response to the eighteenth-century social realities of poverty and injustice in England, they knew firsthand the fact that God's grace could transform people and communities. To the Wesley brothers, grace was the first and the last word of Christian experience; God's grace inspired preaching, teaching, and worship. "Lost in wonder, love, and praise," they expected pastors to be inspired and energized to share "love divine" in their families, congregations, and political involvements.

Practicing the presence of God in ministry involves developing an awareness of God's graceful and transforming presence in the smallest and largest details of our pastoral day and balancing stressful activities with nurturing ones. The two of us believe that experiencing and sharing wonder, love, and praise are at the heart of the pastor's public ministry as preacher, teacher, and liturgist. In these public roles, and in the private roles of spiritual guidance and pastoral care, pastors are called to be "spirit persons," rabbis, and healers who consistently present and embody a vision of life that enables people to practice God's presence in their own lives.[4] In the spirit of Jesus, pastors are called to mediate God's shalom, the Hebraic-Christian vision of wholeness of people and creation, through their preaching, teaching, and liturgical ministries.

We believe that healthy and life-transforming theology and spirituality must be grounded in the dynamic interplay of three elements: vision, promise, and practice. Pastoral ministry finds its inspiration and direction over the long haul in a lived theology, that is, a compelling and spiritually grounded vision of God's nature and work in the world. Without such a vision, pastors cannot guide their congregations in the quest to experience God's grace, healing, and power in the many diverse moments of life, from celebration to bereavement. Pastors gain confidence and hope in ministry through affirming Jesus's promise that they can accomplish "greater works" as they experience the power of their theological affirmations and vision of reality in daily life (John 14:12); that is, they live by the promise that they will be able to experience the faith they affirm. To energize their theological vision means that pastors make an ongoing commitment to practices that enable them and their communities to experience concretely the God about whom they preach in both the ordinary and the extraordinary moments of everyday life.

The sad reality of homiletical burnout and dispirited teaching, preaching, and worship leadership often reflects consciously held or unexamined negative visions of God's presence in pastors' lives and in the world. In the practice of ministry, our theology can be a matter of life and death for pastors and their congregations. How we pastors view the nature of God, the presence of the Spirit, the ongoing ministry of Christ, the scope of revelation, and the breadth of salvation shapes our public ministry and private preparation in the areas of teaching, preaching, and worship far more than we might imagine. It also surfaces in our private acts of counseling and spiritual direction.

While the two of us recognize and affirm the many theological streams of Christianity as well as the limitations of every theological perspective, including our own process-relational vision, we also affirm that spiritually vital public ministry finds its foundation when one affirms and experiences divine inspiration as an ever-present, dynamic, and intimate reality. Accordingly, our theology of revelation applies as much to a pastor's private practices of contemplation and preparation as to a pastor's public ministry of worship leadership, teaching, and preaching. The two of us believe that spiritually vital preaching, as part of an interwoven call and response within a dynamically evolving faith community, always integrates contemplation and action, preparation and presentation, and the mutually enriching gifts of clergy and laity.

Central to our vision of practical ministerial spirituality is the affirmation that God is present as a force for healing and transformation in every moment of life. As Romans 8:26 notes, the Spirit who inspires us in "sighs too deep for words" also inspires all creation to yearn for the wholeness that God imagines for all things. God is present in each moment of life. The responsibility of each of us is to open and respond to God's invitation to experience wholeness, beauty, and love in our relationships with all creation, whether in our household, congregation, or the vast nonhuman world.

A movement toward shalom, wholeness and justice, in all creation undergirds the pastor's role as teacher, preacher, and liturgist. In his ministry of teaching, preaching, and healing, Jesus wanted all people to experience and share in God's abundant life (John 10:10). Regardless of one's theological understanding of the resurrection, the Easter message proclaims that God is present as the call of the future in the midst of life's dead ends, such as suffering, oppression, abuse, and death. God's resurrection vision, embodied in the risen Jesus and in personal experiences of renewal, rebirth, and creative transformation, continually energizes, revives, and lures us toward our vocation as God's beloved children. Our task is to be God's partners in healing *this* world, even as we anticipate the mysterious and infinite healing power of God's everlasting life.

Such lively resurrection faith calls us to experience life and ministry in terms of abundance rather than scarcity. As the biblical tradition constantly asserts, even in the most desperate situations, God is constantly doing a new thing, bringing worlds into being and imagining alternatives to present situations of suffering and injustice. God is calling us to companionship in imagining and embodying new ways of living God's dream of shalom. The living and relational God calls preachers, teachers, and worship leaders to drink deeply of God's wellspring of constantly refreshing living waters as the inspiration for nurturing their own communities of faith.

One biblical source for a lively, universal, and evolving theory of revelation is the narrative of Paul's sermon at the Athenian Areopagus (Acts 17:16–33). Although Paul boldly witnesses to the transforming power of the life, death, and resurrection of Jesus, he also recognizes a clear continuity of revelation that joins the wisdom of Christianity with the wisdom of Athenian religious pluralism. The "unknown God" of the Athenians is, in fact, the loving creator and parent of Jesus "in whom we live and move and have our being" (Acts 17:23, 28). By invoking Stoic philosophy to undergird the life-changing wisdom of Christ's message and resurrection, Paul affirms that divine revelation is universal despite its variability from culture to culture. Paul recognizes that God is truly *present* in the pluralistic theological and spiritual environment of the Areopagus. Paul affirms that God is inspiring the Athenian philosophers and the public worship of the Athenians, but he also recognizes that the Athenians' experiences of the holy point toward the fullness of God's revelation in Jesus of Nazareth, the Risen One.

In our postmodern, pluralistic, and global era, Paul's Areopagus message is good news, both theologically and spiritually, for those of us who preach regularly. First, it reminds us that the One who is at work in all creation is also inspiring our public as well as our private ministries. What does it mean for us to believe that we pastors "live and move and have our being" as part of God's aim at healing, justice, and transformation for all things? For one thing, as the United Church of Christ motto affirms, it means that God is still speaking in theology, science, literature, medicine, and the quest for justice. But more intimately, it affirms that God is still speaking within our lives, whether we are preparing a sermon, walking our dog, enjoying a cookout, or delivering our Sunday sermons. Inspiration is only a moment away for those who are attentive to the Spirit's presence in the details of their lives.

Second, it reminds us that God's prevenient, or preparatory, grace is always working within the lives of those with whom we minister in public worship. Although pastors may, at times, believe they are preaching to congregants who live in a theological and spiritual wasteland, the doctrine of divine omnipresence asserts that, in dramatic or subtle ways, God is touching the spirits of everyone who enters the sanctuary. The two of us believe that in this democracy of revelation there is a God-ward movement in every life. All sermons are best delivered dialogically in spirit, if not literally, to people who have already experienced, but need to become more consciously aware of, God's good news in the depths of their hearts.

When we pastors look out on our congregations, we are invited to imagine God whispering words of grace and challenge not only *to* but also *through* the recalcitrant church board member, the recently bereaved spouse, the uncertain and questioning youth, and the recently laid off autoworker. The word of God echoes not only through the sanctuary in hymns of praise and in proclaiming the gospel but also in the congregational announcements and the inner reflections of the pastor as she prepares to give the opening prayer. We are not alone in receiving divine guidance; we are part of a community of revelation that nurtures and calls forth our own calling as ministers of Word and Sacrament.

Third, living by a sense of the universality of divine inspiration is good news that can transform us as pastors as well as transform our congregations. It means that while every preacher and worship leader is called to faithful excellence and healthy professional and personal boundaries in her or his ministry, she or he is not fully responsible for the spiritual growth of the congregation. God is already at work, whispering within each word the pastor speaks, inspiring the congregation to experience God's blessings and challenges in a personal and intimate way. Preachers can speak words of grace and challenge precisely because such words are not all about the preacher. We can trust the collective impact of Scripture, song, spoken words, and caring and justice-seeking deeds to transform lives because God is in the midst of the community, seeking the wholeness and transformation of everyone present, including the pastor. This lively community touched by God, even when they are unaware of it, eliminates any preacher and congregation separation or dualism.

Liberated from overfunctioning in our roles as preacher, teacher, and worship leader, we pastors can truly experience the grace of holy interdependence. As important as our preaching is to the spiritual growth of congregations, our words are but one factor in the present and future spiritual growth of congregants. Our faithful preparation and worship leadership enables the community as a whole and each person in attendance to experience consciously God's subtle and ever-present call to personal and global healing. We believe that the creativity with which we pastors approach sermons, class sessions, and liturgies is part of a much wider creativity that works not only through our congregational leadership but also in the hearts and minds of all who gather for worship and study. God is with us; divine energy sustains us; divine creativity inspires us.

Preaching, Teaching, and Transformation

We who hold the office of minister of word and sacrament, to use the language of some denominations, are given the responsibility to share the gospel so that congregants may experience the fullness of God in their lives, discover the life-transforming presence of Christ, discern the guidance of the Spirit, find comfort in times of uncertainty and pain, and commit themselves to becoming God's companions in the quest for shalom in their local and global communities. Such an awesome task should both inspire and humble those of us who teach and preach. During an emerging Christianity workshop Bruce was leading, one Church of the Brethren pastor noted the awesome responsibility of preaching: "Virtually every Sunday morning, and often throughout the week, I say to myself, 'Who am I to speak for God? What words can I say that will make a difference to my faith community?' But, I also say to myself, 'I've been called to this task! And, while I may not be the most inspirational preacher, God will help me find words and God will direct my humble reflections to those who need to hear them this morning!'"

Each preaching occasion is an opportunity to receive and give inspiration. Each sermon is an opportunity for the pastor to awaken to divine guidance and experience the gospel in a new way from the moment he or she turns to the lectionary or imagines the topic for Sunday's message.

We believe that lively and fresh preaching week after week is inspired by what we call the "Forrest Gump Principle." As you may recall, Forrest Gump's rather synchronous journey was inspired by his mother's words, "Life was like a box of chocolates. You never know what you're gonna get." As he prepares to read the lectionary readings for the week, Bruce feels a sense of homiletical adventure as he wonders, "What will the readings be for this week? Where will the Scriptures lead me? How will I share them on Saturday night or Sunday morning?" Open to the unexpected revelations of God in the three-year lectionary cycle, Bruce experiences joy and inspiration even in the busiest weeks at the seminary and in his congregation, whether he is preparing for the sermon ahead or writing lectionary commentaries for Process and Faith, a program of the Center for Process Studies, Claremont, California.[5] By contrast, Kate feels a bit of trepidation as she approaches her sermon preparation; but is flush with extraverted joyful anticipation about sharing her reflections when she finishes.

Sadly, many pastors are victims of homiletical burnout. What is intended to be an act of joyful celebration becomes a necessary evil in the life of the preacher. The boredom and fatigue some preachers experience is contagious. Their dispirited preaching contributes to dispirited worship and superficial theological reflection among congregants. As Swiss theologian Karl Barth noted, "If it were toilsome and dull for ministers to do their Sunday work, how could they expect their congregation and the world to find it refreshing?"[6] While repetition is important in the spiritual life, repetition can be deadening for preachers when we forget the resources of divine inspiration in our congregation and among our colleagues in ministry. We pastors are also called to be artists of the spirit who create in partnership with God, other preachers, and lay leaders, and in the process we develop new ways of expressing ancient wisdom in our pluralistic and constantly changing postmodern world.

In our own congregation, Disciples United Community Church in Lancaster, Pennsylvania, we have found new energy for preaching by utilizing congregational *lectio divina* (holy reading) in the sermon and by concluding most sermons with the words "God is still speaking" as an invitation to congregants to recognize and share God's inspiration in their own lives. In so doing, preaching becomes an act of the whole community, young and old, which inspires the preacher and the congregation alike.

The early church theologian Irenaeus recognized that God seeks wholeness and abundant life for all creation. Perhaps his best-remembered words are "The glory of God is a person who is fully alive." What would it be like for you to become a fully alive preacher whose sermon preparation and preaching arises from and contributes to your spiritual growth and ministerial vocation and to the shared collective inspiration of everyone in the congregation? Our experience is that such lively and inspiring preaching over the long haul is the result of the preacher's commitment to practicing the presence of God in the whole of her or his ministry in a way that has distinct personal and corporate dimensions. While there are many paths to experiencing God in sermon preparation and delivery, we suggest the following practices for preachers: (1) listening for God's inspiration, (2) listening to your life, (3) praying your study, (4) taking your sermon for a walk, (5) cultivating creativity, and (6) praying with your congregation. These practices can enliven and inspire your preaching to such a degree that, with Eric Liddell, Olympic sprinter and protagonist of the film *Chariots of Fire*, we postmodern preachers can exclaim, "I believe God made me for a purpose ... and when I [preach] I feel [God's] pleasure."

Listening for God

Throughout Christian history, theologians have affirmed two "books" of revelation—the written word of Holy Scripture and the living, breathing word of Christ in human life and all creation. Our seeking to experience the dynamic interplay of divine revelation's universality and intimacy, we believe, is the ultimate source of our ability to practice God's presence consistently in ministry. Even as pastors seek to experience God everywhere, the unique and decisive revelation of God in Jesus's life, teachings, healings, death, and resurrection and the historical revelation of God's followers, recorded in Hebraic and Christian scriptures, hold great power as a source of transformation for preachers and their congregations. God is speaking a new word and doing a new thing in our place and time, but this new and lively word remains grounded in God's uniquely revealing presence in Jesus of Nazareth and the texts of Scripture. Thus, whenever we pick up the Scriptures to prepare for a sermon, we are not only experiencing Forrest Gump's sense of expectancy at the surprise in the box of scriptural chocolates that awaits us but also opening our lives to the ongoing revelation of the living God in our specific time and place.

Our experience is that the preacher's spiritual formation finds a wellspring of living revelation, initially, in opening to silent listening for God's creative word. As Psalm 46:10 affirms, "Be still, and know that I am God." Pastors can and should take time to listen for the breath of God within their every breath and the word of God in their spoken or unspoken words, no matter how busy their lives may be. All pastors can claim the experience of the women and men whom Jesus breathed upon as he said, "Receive the Holy Spirit" (John 20:22), because just as God's hands are our hands, God's breath is our breath.

As your preaching week begins, your first challenge is to pause for preparation. In so doing, we invite you let go of yesterday's revelations in order to experience God's revelation for today and tomorrow. As you slowly read the passages for the upcoming Sunday, you may ask the question "What new thing will God reveal in my life, my congregation, and the world?" and then take time to listen to the response. Before you focus analytically on the scripture for the week and collect your commentaries and online resources, we suggest that you pause, notice, awaken, and open to God's word in your life and your faith community's life.

Both of us have found the Benedictine practice of *lectio divina* helpful in our own sermon and classroom preparation. While pastors may not have hours to contemplate God's voice in the words of Scripture, we suggest a streamlined form of *lectio divina* that can transform your life and preaching. As you begin your preparation, take time simply to breathe in the quiet inspiration of God. When you feel a sense of calm alertness, take a few moments to read the scripture lessons slowly twice, with a sense of openness and expectation. As you read the lectionary texts or ponder passages you have previously chosen for the upcoming Sunday, the practice of *lectio divina* helps you choose which text truly speaks to you and to your congregation, either by challenging your faith and lifestyle, awakening you to a new insight, or nurturing a sense of comfort and peace.

The following spiritual practice may be helpful to you. If a particular text speaks to you, read it slowly over again as if you are reading it for the first time. You may choose to read it aloud to listen to the sounds of the words and to read it silently to let it soak into your spirit. After you have read the text a few times, pause and hold the intention of noticing the words and images that flow into your consciousness. If a particular word or image particularly speaks to you, focus on that image or word as an echo of God's voice in your life. Let that unique word fill your awareness.

Over the next few days, we invite you to take twenty to thirty minutes each day to live with the text about which you intend to preach, contemplatively breathing, praying the insights you receive, asking God's guidance for relating them to your congregation, and opening to further insights. More than once, a pastor has protested when we make this suggestion with excuses such as, "I don't have time to spend an hour praying my sermon in this way. I barely have time to pick up a commentary anymore." Don't believe it. Our prayerfulness opens us to abundant *kairos* time in the midst of swiftly moving *chronos* time. We believe that you don't have time *not* to pray the scriptures of the week.

If you can't spend half an hour each day dedicated to this process, take ten or fifteen minutes if you are able, in combination with a repetitive task such as washing the dishes, folding laundry, or making the bed. Kate likes to reflect on her sermons while pulling weeds or working in our garden. As pastors, we are called to be people of prayer who touch our spiritual depths and share them with those to whom we minister. Times of prayer and meditation are *not* optional in preaching preparation. As one pastor notes, "When I use *lectio divina* as part of my sermon preparation, I know God will give me the insights I need. I always look forward to the next week's sermon, because it gives me an opportunity to deepen my faith while I'm preparing to help my parishioners deepen their own faith."

Listening to Your Life

Reflection, spiritual autobiography, and journaling can open you to what your own life is saying. When Bruce teaches courses in *spiritual autobiography* to laypeople and pastors, he invites them to explore twin sources of God's presence within their lives described by the phrases "listen to your life" and "let your life speak," coined by Frederick Buechner and Parker Palmer, respectively.[7] The practice of spiritual autobiography involves, first of all, simple awareness and remembrance of God moments in your life, and then recording those moments on the printed page; in poetry, art, music, dance; or in any other media that expresses your spiritual adventure. In so doing, we discover ourselves to be "bards of the Holy Ghost," as Ralph Waldo Emerson described the soon-to-be ordained pastors he addressed at a Harvard Divinity School graduation. We are poets and artists of life and ministry, expressing God's presence uniquely, fallibly, and beautifully in our time and place.

Spiritual autobiography reminds us that we can experience God's intimate revelation in the intricacies of our own lives and encounters. When pastors truly listen to their lives, they can experience with Jacob's insight, following his dream of a ladder of angels going from earth to heaven and back again, that God "is in this place—and I did not [at the time] know it!" (Gen. 28:16). Pastors who practice the art of spiritual autobiography can discover a surprising parallel between God's presence in the women and men of the Bible and God's presence in their own lives. As one pastor noted following a workshop on spiritual autobiography, "I feel a lot like Esther as I face the challenges of being a pastor in a changing urban neighborhood. I'd like to hide or remain silent. But, like Esther, God has called me here 'for just such a time as this'" (Est. 4:14). In remembering and affirming God's call in their lives, pastors can claim their role as storytellers of the Spirit, witnessing to God's presence in their lives as a way of inviting others to tell their own stories of faith.

Pastors who look for God's presence in the ordinary as well as the dramatic moments of their lives soon discover that their own lives are truly interesting and that they have something to say. They recognize that their ministries are part of a much greater holy adventure than they had previously imagined.

According to Edward Wimberly, professor of pastoral care and counseling at the Interdenominational Theological Center in Atlanta, Georgia, many African American pastors recite their call story with their congregations on a yearly basis.[8] Remembering our call and sharing it with others not only awakens congregants to God's presence and call in their own lives but also feeds the fire of spiritual vitality necessary for healthy, vital, spirit-centered ministry over the long haul. When we recall how we have lived out our call to ministry, it helps us become more aware of God's lively presence in our lives and the lives of our congregants. We discover that God, who began a good work in our lives when we were called to ministry, will bring our vocational call to fulfillment (Phil. 1:6).[9]

Pause a moment and consider your call to ministry. As you listen to your life, take time to remember the moments you experienced God's call. In your recollections, go back as far as possible, inspired by questions such as the following:

1. What was your most joyful childhood experience?
2. When did you first experience God as a reality in your life?
3. How has your experience of God changed over the years? How did you as a child picture God? How do you picture God today? (You may even choose to draw a picture of your childhood and adult images of God.)
4. When did you first experience the reality of death? How did people around you respond to the reality of death?
5. When did you first fall in love? How did you feel?
6. When did you first feel called to ordained ministry and spiritual leadership in the church? How did you experience this call?
7. How have you experienced your call being affirmed?
8. What has been your greatest joy in ministry?
9. What has been your greatest challenge in ministry?
10. How do you most vividly experience God's presence in your ministry today?

Reflecting on these questions opens the door to scores of other questions and recollections. We encourage you to reflect on these in your quiet times and, perhaps, journal about them. Despite the challenges of ministry, practicing spiritual autobiography awakens us pastors to wisdom akin to that of the character George Bailey in the 1946 movie *It's a Wonderful Life*. We discover our wonderful life of ministry within the day-to-day challenges and frustrations of being a pastor. As one student reflected on his spiritual autobiography in a doctor of ministry course at Wesley Theological Seminary, Washington, DC, he rejoiced at his discovery of the many apparently unimportant encounters that had been life transforming for himself and his congregants: "I never realized how many lives I've touched in my ministry. When I feel depressed about the struggles of day-to-day ministry, I take time to review my life story and find both consolation and inspiration."

The practice of *spiritual journaling* can also be a powerful tool for discovering anew the living presence of God in our ministries. Kate has kept a spiritual journal for most of her adult life. Over the years, her thoughts and questions have often been reworded as prayers of intercession and supplication. Spiritual journaling is a daily reminder of God's call within our lives, the many wonders of each day, and the adventure that is lived out in our quotidian joys and sorrows. As one journal writer notes, "Journaling grounds me in God's daily blessings even on the most difficult days. As the Bible says, God's mercies are new every morning. When I journal I realize that God is sustaining and inspiring me, whether or not I am consciously aware of it." Another pastor says that "journaling reminds me of the richness of my own experience and gives me a wealth of ideas for sermons. More than that, journaling reminds me that God is also at work in the ordinary lives of people in my congregation."

Truly, when we listen deeply to our lives, we can experience a holy adventure that deepens both our ministry and our sermon preparation. We begin to listen more closely to the joys and sorrows of people in our congregations. Our attentiveness to the daily joys and sorrows of their lives inspires and guides our own preaching practices and illustrations—framed anonymously, of course.

Praying Your Study

"Pastors have studies and not offices," Bruce often tells seminary students and participants in ministerial excellence and spiritual formation programs. The two of us believe that the current use of the word *office* reveals a profoundly unhelpful popular shift away from understanding the vocation of minister as rabbi, teacher, and spirit person to administrator, program manager, professional counselor, and functional CEO. Although we will explore the spiritual aspects of administration and pastoral care in chapters 3 and 4, we maintain that keeping an emphasis on preaching, healing, and teaching roles in ministry challenges pastors to reclaim their core spiritual vocation as spiritual guides and teachers within their congregations.

Most pastors complain about insufficient time for study and reflection. As Steve, a newly ordained United Church of Christ pastor, confesses, "When I was in seminary, I looked forward to being able to follow my preaching professor's counsel to spend an hour of study for every minute of preaching. But the realities of parish life make it impossible for me to spend more than a few hours a week in sermon preparation and research. I may never spend more than ten hours a week on study and preparation, but something needs to change if I am to be a good teacher for my congregation." Andrea, a United Methodist pastor, also notes that "Amid the day-to-day challenges of running the church, I barely have time to sit down for more than an hour at a time to study, much less pray. I get a lot of my sermon ideas from online lectionary helps and sermons. I wish I could be more creative in my preaching and teaching."

Some, however, manage to integrate study into their everyday rhythm of pastoral duties. Despite the challenges of being the busy pastor of a midsized congregation, Barbara Blaisdell, former pastor of First Christian Church (Disciples of Christ) in Concord, California, asserts that she needs to read constantly to keep her mind stimulated for the week-to-week task of writing several pages of creative reflections for the Sunday sermon.[10] As an antidote to hurried preparation that manifests itself in superficial preaching and homiletical burnout, she honors study as a form of spiritual formation and takes seriously her calling as rabbi of her congregation. For many pastors, this honoring of study as a necessary spiritual practice involves taking a serious look at how they spend their time and prioritize their commitments.

As you look at your own week, do you block out time in advance for study and preaching preparation? Or do you frequently drop your disciplines of study and preparation in deference to your congregation's seemingly more pressing pastoral and administrative needs, regardless of their importance to the church's life?

We believe that preaching and teaching take *time* and *leisure*. Ministers who choose to cultivate their spirituality amid the regular tasks of preaching must set aside time each day for study. When the two of us review our schedules at the beginning of each month or each week, we consciously block out several hours each week for study and sermon preparation. This time, like our prayer time, becomes nonnegotiable, except in the case of authentic pastoral and administrative emergencies. Otherwise, precious time for study is swallowed up by the amoebic nature of ministerial tasks. In her last full-time pastorate, Kate accomplished this commitment by choosing *not* to come into the church office until 10:00 AM. As an easily distracted extravert, she needed the relative seclusion of her home to study and pray. Bruce, who is more introverted by nature, meditates, prays, studies, and writes every day by rising a few hours before the rest of the household.

Regarding study as a spiritual discipline central to your teaching, preaching, and spiritual life requires having several flexible approaches to what we refer to as praying your study. First, we suggest reading widely and regularly. Breadth and depth of teaching and preaching is dependent upon a pastor's study of texts and articles unrelated as well as related to the weekly topical or lectionary texts. The two of us have profited from regularly selecting fiction and nonfiction texts on the best-sellers list as well as the classics, recently released texts in theology and spiritual formation, and books of art and poetry. We often ask laypeople what they are reading and then integrate these texts into our reading lists. Kate leads a book group in our congregation, which not only stimulates reflection and builds fellowship within the congregation but also helps her gain insights into where the congregants are intellectually and spiritually.

Second, take time to meditate on the scriptures of the week, organize your own images and thoughts, and claim your own personal experience and wisdom *before* you consult the commentaries as a means of gaining a wider perspective and evaluating your initial prayerful insights. Preaching and teaching is a creative tapestry of many voices—tradition, current scholarship, your congregational context, lectionary commentaries—woven together by the integrity and richness of your own pastoral artistry. Stature in preaching emerges when we embrace contrasting viewpoints in light of our own personal wisdom.

Third, the importance of taking time to pray throughout your entire process of study and preparation cannot be stressed enough. As you open Scripture or a commentary, take a deep, gentle breath as an act of opening to God's Spirit. As you turn on your computer or pick up a pad of paper upon which to take notes, let these acts be accompanied by a conscious intention that God will be present in each word, guiding you to write and speak words of healing, challenge, wisdom, and transformation to your congregation.

Did you know that each year, the average pastor writes the equivalent of two to three hundred pages of sermons? This amounts to writing more than a book a year. Can you imagine what your sermons would like if you gathered them into a book each year? Would they hold together, showing a creative flow of inspiration and thoughtfulness that reflects your own personal and pastoral integrity? Inspirational preaching that embraces the whole of your life emerges when you take time to see the big picture of your preaching as well as the unique message of the Sunday-to-Sunday texts. Seeking this sort of perspective and integrity promotes personal and professional stature. Accordingly, the spiritual formation of preachers should always involve a commitment to looking ahead at least several weeks in order to discern the patterns of God's inspiration in the lectionary or topical texts.

Praying our times of study inspires pastors to see theological reflection as a form of prayer. One of the greatest challenges we pastors face is to claim our own theological voice and then find care-full ways to share that voice with our communities of faith. We recognize that, typically, even the most creative pastors require a few years of preaching and study beyond seminary to claim intellectually and spiritually their own theological voice. In this spirit, experienced pastor and pastoral counselor Jack Good appropriately notes that pastors are harmed spiritually when they fail to preach their deepest theological insights in order to fit into their congregational ethos. Indeed, Good asserts that his conversations with clergy "make him confident that one of the reasons for the high dropout rate is the conflict between what they have come to believe and what they feel safe to say in pulpits and church school classrooms."[11] Some pastors, Good notes, may even revert to their less theologically informed preseminary theological formulae in order to fit into their congregational ethos.

While we recognize that some pastors fit Good's description of homiletical cowardice, laziness, and dishonesty, we believe that most pastors recognize that spirit-centered and theologically sound preaching and teaching promote well-being for both the pastor and her or his congregation. The best antidote to "dishonest" preaching is simply taking time to develop your own personal theology in prayerful conversation with Scripture, tradition, reason, experience, culture, and trusted colleagues and people with whom you minister. But in this postmodern time of rapid scientific and social change, developing a theology you can believe in and hold to in your preaching and teaching is not enough. You also need to explore creative approaches to sharing your faith and theology so that your congregants can articulate their faith and beliefs themselves.

Bridge building and translation for contemporary settings and cultures are essential in effective preaching, ministry, and pastoral care. When we pastors prayerfully listen to congregants' experiences as well as our own experiences, we discover important points of contact between our own spiritual yearnings and the deep but often unspoken spiritual desires of congregants. In this mutual listening, we learn to formulate a relational theology that joins personal and corporate theological integrity with preaching and teaching styles and content that heals, transforms, challenges, and comforts the congregations to which we are called. To be sure, such bridge building takes time and leisure both in exploring the great insights of our faith tradition and in the consequent creative translation of these insights into innovative images and ideas for congregational edification and transformation. Ultimately, it requires listening and trusting the subtle stirrings of the Spirit in our experiences and the experiences of congregants.

A fourth method for praying your study in preparation for preaching is a day-long theological retreat. Bruce has found this helpful and takes a day each year in which he reflects on his central theological beliefs. During such retreats, he considers the following: (1) his nonnegotiable theological affirmations, (2) his spiritual and personal growth in light of these affirmations during the past year, and (3) new insights with which he is currently wrestling. Then he takes time to consider how he can share his faith honestly in ways that will benefit our congregation and his students while maintaining his integrity and credibility. Such retreats can nurture your spiritual and intellectual life and add depth and breadth to your preaching.

As rabbis in our congregations, we pastors find spiritual energy and inspiration as we continually make a commitment to love God with our minds as well as our souls and hearts. Practicing the presence of God in preaching and teaching provides an ongoing wellspring of creativity, vitality, and spiritual depth that ripples out to transform every aspect of ministry.

Taking Your Sermon for a Walk

Throughout our trilogy of books on ministerial spiritual formation, health, and excellence, we have stressed the importance of spiritual, intellectual, and physical movement in ministry.

Judaism and Christianity are faiths that celebrate the movement of God and God's people in nature and history. The God of the Hebraic peoples inspires and guides the personal and communal pilgrimages of the Israelites. While not confined in space and time, the Hebraic God is a God of adventure, novelty, creativity, and motion. In its account of the birth of Jesus, Christian faith affirms God's companionship with people on the move—Mary and Joseph were exiles and immigrants; the shepherds rushed to Bethlehem; and the magi followed a star and a dream. It is no accident that the disciples experienced the risen Christ on a walk to Emmaus. The risen Christ walks with us and guides our adventures as faithful and creative companions of the way, always inviting us to expect to entertain strangers, and angels unaware, at every twist and turn of the road of ministry (Heb. 13:2). In the lively and constantly changing postmodern world, pastors must be prepared to do ministry on the move, engaging new ideas as well as exploring new venues for outreach and mission.

The very act of movement, even if only in our imagination, enlivens and strengthens our bodies and sets our spirits free to experience new perspectives on the Scriptures and our journeys as pastors. In reflecting on her practice of preaching, Linda Clader, an Episcopal priest and professor of homiletics at Church Divinity School of the Pacific in Berkeley, California, notes, "In between these times of sitting in the study, I have one other intentional activity connected with my preaching: I take walks. . . . [In walking, I am] taking some time away from the sermon to let the material simmer, to let the creative juices run un-channeled, to let the Holy Spirit move in and stir things up."[12] In her forty-minute preaching walks, Clader notes that she speaks and listens to God and prays for inspiration and the right words for her congregation.[13] Disciples of Christ minister Barbara Blaisdell agrees that "a long walk will do amazing things to clarify what I have to say."[14]

Bruce regularly takes his sermon out for a walk. As he walks in our West Lancaster neighborhood or across the Franklin and Marshall College campus adjoining Lancaster Theological Seminary, he asks God's wisdom, present in both conscious insights and unconscious intuitions, to guide his reflections and writing. Bruce takes seriously the reality of God's ever-present inspiration as an invitation to trust God's presence within the unconscious realm of hunches, synchronous encounters, dreams, and insights. He believes that the darkness of the unconscious mediates divine light to those who have awakened to its wisdom. Unlike Bruce, the more extraverted Kate enjoys letting her sermon ideas, thoughts, and prayers bubble as she chatters away on her daily walks with Bruce. (Yes, Bruce usually takes two or three walks a day!)

Whether we pastors walk our sermons, take them out for a jog, or simply imagine the text emerging unhindered in our lives, movement liberates our spirits to embrace God's ever-creative inspiration flowing through our lives. Moving in the spirit breaks through intellectual, emotional, and spiritual blocks that stand in the way of our preaching. Jana Childers, Presbyterian minister and professor of homiletics and speech communication at San Francisco Theological Seminary, affirms that "repetitive large muscle activity can help you overcome your writer's block.... It dissipates anxiety and quiets the conscious mind."[15]

Preaching is a holistic process that embraces mind, body, and spirit. While we do not prescribe one particular way of moving with the spirit, we invite you to take the scripture texts along with you as you engage in some form of gentle exercise. In the spirit of *lectio divina*, you may reflect on a single word, phrase, or image as you walk. You may choose simply to let your mind wander as you gaze upon your familiar neighborhood scene or distant mountain vistas while hiking. You may also ask your unconscious to work creatively as you enjoy the fluid interplay of body, mind, and spirit while swimming, jogging, walking, or even dancing to the words of Scripture. On your own Emmaus journey, we believe that you will find God in the movement.

Cultivating Creativity

Practicing the presence of God holistically in preaching, teaching, and worship involves our openness to God's creative and transforming presence in our personal and professional lives. The biblical story portrays God as responding creatively and gracefully to the often wayward adventures of the children of Israel and Jesus's first followers through dreams, visions, synchronous encounters, and inspiring moments. We believe that such urgings still regularly call us to go forth from familiar places toward uncharted spiritual frontiers.

The philosopher Alfred North Whitehead once noted that higher organisms originate novelty to match the novelty of their environments.[16] Accordingly, the spiritually alive pastor seeks to cultivate a spirit of adventure and creativity in her or his approach to preaching, teaching, and worship leadership to be sure. Imagination is a central element of preaching and teaching. Before we can invite our congregations on a journey with Abraham and Sarah or Mary Magdalene or the apostle Paul, we must cultivate the spirit of adventure in our own lives and ministerial activities.

One of the most fertile pathways to creativity we have found is by integrating art and literature. Whether or not we admit it, we are all artists and poets of the Spirit. No one experiences the world from our vantage point; nor does anyone respond to the same events exactly as we do. However you name it, most spiritually alive pastors see themselves as artists in partnership with the Divine Artist.

But how do we liberate the spiritual artist within so that we might inspire creative partnership in worship, teaching, and preaching with our congregations? Once again, the inner and outer journeys of ministry flourish in a dynamic, interdependent relationship. We can become artists of the spirit simply by playing and praying through our ministry. Inspired by his colleague at Lancaster Theological Seminary Anabel Proffitt, associate professor of educational ministry, Bruce has integrated artistic projects such as collages, drawing, and poetry in his doctoral classes at Wesley Theological Seminary and masters level classes at Lancaster Theological Seminary. While participants often giggle nervously or joke about such a "juvenile" project when they begin working on collages related to their spiritual autobiography or sense of vocation, within a few minutes they are so engrossed in the project that they complain when Bruce signals that only a few minutes remain. An artist by nature, Kate has always done this within spiritual direction and pastoral care. Inspired by the work of her spiritual director, who is herself a visual artist as well as spiritual guide, Kate often invites participants in Lancaster Theological Seminary's ministerial excellence and spiritual formation groups to explore spiritual autobiography through watercolor. As they reflect on their collage or watercolor painting, participants are often surprised to learn something important about their current practice of ministry, sense of vocation, or future professional or personal adventures. Playing with paper, colors, crayons, clay, or words opens us to new avenues of inspiration as we weave together insights from both right and left hemispheres of the brain and conscious and unconscious wisdom through moments of holy creativity and revelation.

So, too, the lively preacher explores the interplay of Scripture, her own experience, and world events through a similar process of artistic creative synthesis. Translating complicated theological doctrines related to the Trinity, justice, the relationship of Jesus with God, or the reality of suffering within your worshiping community is an act of theological imagination in which words and concepts from the academic world are shaped and molded into ordinary language and everyday imagery. Relating current events to lectionary readings also requires an artistic touch that leaves room for personal creativity of those who hear the sermon. Spiritually vital preaching invites the listener to "overhear" the gospel, to quote homiletics professor Fred Craddock, in your own spiritual journey and exploration of the text. In so doing, the text comes alive within your own creative process.

This being said, creativity and improvisation in preaching, teaching, and worship are not accidental but clearly the result of openness to possibility and adventure in our own lives and ministries. Mike Graves suggests, in the spirit of Julia Cameron's *The Artist's Way*, that pastors make a habit of scheduling regular preacher's dates in which they explore poetry, classics, and children's literature and participate in book groups as ways of stimulating creativity.[17] In this same spirit, we recommend visits to art galleries and museums, gardening, pottery, watercoloring, beachcombing, hiking, symphonies, jazz sessions, and poetry readings. If your preaching and teaching arise out of the interplay of Scripture, theology, prayer, and artistry, then creative and lively preaching will ensue. Practicing the presence of God in cocreativity with God awakens us to an unending holy adventure in which each sunrise brings surprises, challenges, and opportunities for newness of life.

Wonder and Worship

As we mentioned in the introduction, Bruce begins each day with an affirmation, "This is the day God has made, and I will rejoice and be glad in it!" (Ps. 118:24, paraphrased), and a question, "What exciting thing will God ask of me today?" Bruce's morning ritual captures the essence of vital personal devotion and congregational worship—the interplay of praise, wonder, gratitude, and response. For both pastor and congregation, life-transforming worship joins awe and wonder, both of which are inspired by God's Spirit moving freshly and creatively in our lives.[18] Christian worship, according to Gordon Lathrop, "orients its participants in the world" and joins worship and ethics, liturgy and daily life.[19]

Whether in personal devotion or public worship, our hymns of praise and gratitude arise from our willingness to seek God's presence in the ordinary as well as the dramatic moments of life. When we let our faith bubble up in moments of wonder and thankfulness, our practices resemble those of the Aboriginal spirit persons whose song lines create a spiritual geography that orients their lives. Those moments arise and give us vision and perspective from which to experience God's presence and call in the totality of our personal and professional lives.

As a repetitive act of pastoral ministry, preparing for and leading public worship may become routine and dispirited for pastor and congregation alike, but these acts may also be an invitation to accompany God on a holy adventure, strewn with challenges and surprises during the course of every day. As we deepen our experience of the living and creative God, our liturgical preparation and leadership deepens and grows in inspiration.

The purpose of this section, "Wonder and Worship," is to inspire ministers to join personal and public worship as they seek to awaken to God's call and respond in ways that bring beauty and healing to the earth. We will explore four aspects of practicing the presence of God in worship leadership: (1) cultivating wonder, (2) transforming praise, (3) living by thanksgiving, and (4) praying with our bodies.

Cultivating Wonder

As he imagined the wonders of the universe, we suspect that the psalmist experienced the same awe that twenty-first century people experience as they meditate upon photographs from the Hubble telescope: "When I look at your heavens, the work of your fingers, the moon and the stars that you have established; what are human beings that you are mindful of them, mortals that you care for them?" (Ps. 8:3–4).

Creating galaxy upon galaxy and rejoicing in the creative process that has brought forth humankind amidst the vast universe, divine wisdom calls to us to see beauty and wonder in the smallest events and in the grand panorama of galaxy creation and cosmic evolution (Prov. 8:1, 22–31). Awestruck by the magnificence of the universe, the psalmist remembers that his own life is a creative synthesis of universality and intimacy. He discovers that the creative God is also inspiring creativity in humankind: "Yet you have made [human beings] a little lower than God, and crowned them with glory and honor" (Ps. 8:5).

The two of us believe that individuals can experience each moment as an epiphany, a revealing of God, in which the holistic wisdom of God shines forth, whether in the birth of a child, preparing a memorial service or a wedding, the touch of a lover, or, as Julian of Norwich notes, the very existence of a hazelnut. Divine possibility that brings forth oaks from acorns and apples from seeds is ready to bring forth something of beauty in our own lives and ministries. Julian of Norwich observes, "God showed me something small, no bigger than a hazelnut, lying in the palm of my hand. . . . I was amazed that it could last, for I thought because of its littleness it would suddenly have fallen into nothing. And I was answered in my understanding: It lasts and always will because God loves it; and thus everything has being through the love of God."[20]

Even for people such as Kate who struggle with low-grade depression throughout their lives, wonder, love, and praise characterize vital, spirit-centered, transforming ministry over the long haul. While we cannot create wonder entirely by our own efforts, we can put ourselves in the position to experience wonder by choosing to pause, notice, open ourselves, and awaken to the awe and wonder of God's presence through all our senses and in all our experiences. Annie Dillard notes in her book *Pilgrim at Tinker Creek* that the whole world is "strewn with magic pennies," the surprising wonders of God's love.[21] Her words convict us as we ask, "But who notices a penny?" We forget that omnipresence means that the loving, graceful, healing, and liberating God is everywhere and in everything.

The same practices that inspire your teaching and preaching awaken you to God's presence in your worship preparation and leadership, whether in private preparation or public proclamation. Taking time to practice the presence of God in worship invites you to taste and see that God is good (Ps. 34:8). In other words, if on a day-to-day basis, you take time to practice attuning all your senses to God's movements in your life and in the world, then we believe that you will have daily opportunities to pause awhile to notice God's presence through taste, sight, smell, touch, and hearing. You *can* actually worship God yourself as you lead worship. In your worship leadership, you can become an apostle of wonder and grace as you proclaim through multisensory liturgies the creative-responsive love of God.[22]

You can train your senses as a worship leader by following the advice you probably heard in childhood about crossing the street—stop, look, and listen for God's revealing in all things, and then respond by claiming your vocation as revealers of the wonders you have seen and heard. Amid the manifold daily tasks of ministry and especially the structured chaos of Sunday mornings, we invite you to make an effort to remind yourself, perhaps through a breath prayer or a moment of quiet in your study before the service, to look for one thing among the many duties of ministerial leadership—the healing and graceful presence of God, which is your greatest source of insight, inspiration, and energy in worship, teaching, and preaching.

Transforming Praise

Wonder, praise, and gratitude constitute the holy trinity of worship that inspires, heals, transforms, and challenges pastors and their communities in their quest to be God's companions mending the world. To cultivate these virtues is to cultivate the "radical amazement," that Rabbi Abraham Joshua Heschel sees as the heart of religious experience.[23]

Praise is an essential spiritual practice for ministers in their worship preparation and leadership. Praise centers and grounds us in divine love that brings worlds into being, guides the evolution of galaxies and people, and breathes new life through all creation and in every situation. Authentic praise is not a matter of stroking the divine ego or perpetuating hierarchical understandings of the divine-human relationship, but the recognition that God is the lively, intimate, and creative reality from which each moment of life emerges. Always inspiring, guiding, and creating our lives moment by moment and breath by breath, the Divine Artist works within the materials of our lives bringing forth beauty, character, and virtue.

Praise and gratitude are the public acts of wonder and appreciation for all that God is and all that God is doing in our lives and the universe. In this paraphrase of Psalm 148 and 150, all creation, human and nonhuman, is called to praise God (148:1–4, 11–12; 150:6):

> Praise God! Praise God in the heavens; praise God in the heights!
> Praise God, all God's angels; praise God, all God's host!
> Praise God, sun and moon; Praise God, all you shining stars!
> Praise God, you highest heavens, and you waters above the heavens!
>   . . .
> Rulers of the earth and all peoples, princes and rulers of all the earth!
> Young men and women alike, old and young together! . . .
> Let everything that breathes praise God! Praise God!

Praise transforms pastors and congregations alike by turning our vision from the crisis of the present moment to the ever-present goodness of God. Like a good song or psalm, praise lifts our spirits and awakens new energies for personal and congregational health and transformation. While praise does not deny the realities of suffering and pain, it reminds us that divine love and creativity will have the final word in our lives and in the world. Praise is an essential antidote to the self-preoccupation and idolatry that often ensnare people, congregations, and communities. Praise reminds us of our radical dependence upon—and interdependence with—God's saving and redeeming grace. Praise reminds us that we are never alone and that God is already supplying and will continue to supply our deepest needs for inspiration, creativity, and strength in times of conflict and despair in our professional and personal lives.

The two of us have found that commitment to practicing praise and thanksgiving takes us beyond ourselves and sweeps us up into the ongoing adventure of the universe and its creator. A spirit of praise enables us to face failure, sickness, and death with confidence that nothing can separate us from the love of God and that in Christ we are more than conquerors (Rom. 8:37–39). When we think of the transforming power of praise, we remember the service of installation for Sue Zabel as full professor at Wesley Theological Seminary in Washington, DC. Having been recently diagnosed with cancer that would eventually lead to her death, Sue led the seminary community in the final hymn of the service, "Many Gifts, One Spirit":

> God of change and glory, God of time and space,
> When we face the future, give to us your grace.
> In the midst of changing ways,
> Give us still the grace to praise.

As she faced the long and challenging journey that lay before her, Sue could still proclaim "for the giver and the gift, praise, praise, praise."[24]

Along with wonder and love, praise is at the heart of practicing the presence of God in ministry. You can practice life-transforming praise by beginning each day acknowledging

God's creativity and grace and by taking time throughout your day to give God praise and glory for God's ongoing blessings. In those moments when you are overcome by stress and fear, you can recall God's faithfulness from age to age by using creative affirmations that will enable you to live in the divine center amid the changes and challenges of each day. We have used affirmations such as these to cultivate a life-transforming spirit of praise:

> I praise you, God, for the beauty of the sunrise.
> I praise you, God, for your amazing love for me and all creation.
> I praise you, God, for your sustaining presence in my life.
> I praise you, God, for your presence in my family during these difficult times.
> I praise you, God, for calling me to ordained ministry.

Living by Thanksgiving

Gratitude is an essential aspect of practicing the presence of God in ministry and worship leadership. Two thousand years ago, the apostle Paul recognized gratitude as one the primary practices in Christian formation: "Rejoice always, pray without ceasing, give thanks in all circumstances; for this is the will of God in Christ Jesus for you" (1 Thess. 5:16–18).

Thanksgiving is the practice of responsive interdependence. When we give thanks, we recognize the divine abundance from which our lives arise. As ministers, the two of us have been blessed to walk with many people in moments of anguish and joy. While we recognize the many challenges of ministry and congregational life in the postmodern world, we also affirm the blessings that come with the call to ordained ministry in just such a time as this. As pastors, there is no greater blessing than being called to comfort the dying and to give guidance to seekers and "spiritual orphans,"[25] to serve the least of these in the name of Christ, and to awaken people to God's presence in their lives. Through God's grace, we are called to study, bless, heal, and teach. No two days are alike in ministry if we choose to embrace God's presence in our ministry. Surprises wait around every corner.

There is much for which we pastors can be thankful. Although we may work long hours, as pastors we are our fortunate to have, if we so choose, schedules that are flexible enough to enable us to pick up our children from school, meet with friends and colleagues at a coffee shop, or take walks with friends and partners in the midst of a busy day. But beyond that, of course, ordained ministers have the privilege of sharing the good news of Christ's life, teaching, and resurrection. As one experienced American Baptist pastor notes, "In what other profession could a person anoint the sick, pray with new parents, read a theological classic, ponder God's word in Scripture, take an afternoon walk with my wife, and after dinner play volleyball with the youth group, all in the same day!"

Gratitude places the challenges of ministry in perspective. As dispiriting as congregational conflict, diminishing financial resources, culture wars, and decreasing membership may be for some pastors, the practice of regular thanksgiving enables us to experience God's blessings in all the tasks and challenges of ministry. In the wise words of author Anne Lamott, "Gratitude, not understanding, is the secret to joy and equanimity."[26]

While there is no one way to practice thanksgiving in ministry and worship leadership, we suggest that you make a covenant to give thanks for God's blessings at regular intervals throughout the day. Thanksgiving involves the art of mindful awareness—pausing, noticing, and opening—of moments of love, beauty, friendship, and faith. Giving thanks for them as they occur enables us to experience God in the large and small events of life, including the most heartbreaking moments of ministry. We deepen our experience of thanksgiving not only by giving thanks to God throughout each day but also by the practice of "thanks-living," or blessing others in our daily encounters through our words of gratitude to them.

Take a few minutes now to reflect on your experiences of gratitude. Do you regularly give thanks for the ordinary events of your day—waking up, eating, and sharing time with family and friends? Do you give thanks for your calling to ministry and the people to whom you minister? Do you regularly say thank you to those who serve and support you—firefighters, law officers, members of the armed services, clerks, secretaries, colleagues, congregational lay leaders and volunteers? Do you regularly say thank you to your closest friends, family, and relatives?

Praying with Our Bodies

So far, the two of us have focused entirely on what many pastors typically consider the private, preparatory, and contemplative aspects of preaching, teaching, and worship leadership. While there is no ultimate separation between contemplation and action, private and public, or body, mind, and spirit, in a vocational world characterized by relationship and interdependence, we believe that spiritual integrity, wholeness, and vitality in a pastor's life begins with a commitment to practicing God's presence through maintaining physical well-being and wholeness. Our physical well-being shapes the quality of our worship leadership.

In the midst of the busyness of Sunday morning, you can *pause, notice, open, yield and stretch,* and *respond* to God's presence in ways that join mind, body, and spirit. As you prepare to enter the sanctuary, you can take a moment to pray in solitude or with your worship team, choir, or elders. Here we mean a heartfelt prayer, not a perfunctory calling upon a distant deity. You can take a moment to be still with your worship partners to breathe deeply God's presence and to center yourselves before sharing public words of gratitude, praise, and presence with congregants. You can invite your partners in worship leadership to stretch out their open hands as they breathe as a way to open to God's spirit and inspiration in the hour ahead.

When we pick up the microphone or go to the lectern for words of welcome and prayers of awareness and invocation, we both like to pause a moment and breathe deeply from deep in our bellies, allowing divine inspiration to calm, center, and guide us. Our experience is that our own moments of stillness, grounding, and centering enable members of our congregation also to experience the blessings of silence and centering. Finally, we suggest that as you prepare to deliver your sermon, you can also take a moment to breathe deeply. As you breathe deeply, you can see more deeply the people who are gathered for worship, and in inhaling and exhaling, you can experience your spiritual connection to them. As you gaze at your congregation, filled with the spirit, or pneuma, of God, you can truly affirm the words, "Let everything that breathes praise God!"

Practicing the Presence of God in Teaching, Preaching, and Worship

We conclude this chapter with spiritual practices that are intended to awaken your experience of God's presence in the pastoral tasks of teaching, preaching, and worship leadership.

Reading Scripture with Your Whole Self

The psalmist proclaims, "Bless [God], O my soul, and all that is within me, bless [God's] holy name" (Ps. 103:1). We are to love God with all our mind, heart, and strength, as we affirm loving relationships with neighbors near and far. To truly embody the truths of the Scriptures we preach and teach requires imaginative empathy, which is, in the best sense, holistic.

Imagination is essential to faithful and effective pastoral leadership in the areas of preaching, teaching, and worship.

Inspired by the *Spiritual Exercises* of Ignatius of Loyola, written by the founding parent of the Society of Jesus, the Jesuits, pastors can experience the text with all their senses—mind, body, and spirit—as they prepare sermons and worship services.[27] Bruce is grateful for his year-long retreat focused on the *Spiritual Exercises* with Father Jerry Campbell, S.J., who was at the time on the pastoral staff of Holy Trinity Roman Catholic Church in Washington, DC. As a seminarian, Kate first encountered imaginative prayer as a result of her participation in regular contemplative retreats, sponsored by the Disciplined Order of Christ. In these retreats, an Ignatian-style resource, *A Month with the Master*, written by Archie Matson was used as a basis for personal and group meditative experiences.[28] We have adapted the *Spiritual Exercises* of Ignatius of Loyola over the years in our personal spiritual practices as well as the spiritual direction we provide for individuals and groups.

In your practice of imaginatively praying the Scriptures, we invite you to begin with a moment of silent breathing as you open yourself to God's guidance for your life and ministry. Then, take a few moments to read the following passage at least twice with an attitude of prayerful expectation that you will be inspired by God in your meditative prayer.

> The apostles gathered around Jesus, and told him all that they had done and taught. He said to them, "Come away to a deserted place all by yourselves and rest awhile." For many were coming and going, and they had no leisure even to eat. And they went away in the boat to a deserted place by themselves. Now many saw them going and recognized them, and they hurried there on foot from all the towns and arrived ahead of them. As he went ashore, he saw a great crowd; and he had compassion for them, because they were like sheep without a shepherd; and he began to teach them many things (Mark 6:30–34).

Take a moment to reflect on your current ministerial practices. Looking gently at your life, ask yourself the following questions: What are your successes? What are your stresses? What would you like to share with Jesus?

After a moment's silence, visualize yourself and a number of other pastors in conversation with Jesus. Visualize your meeting place. What is it like? Do you recognize any of your companions in ministry?

Imagine Jesus asking each of you to share with him how you are feeling about your ministry. Visualize yourself sharing with Jesus your joys and challenges and your overall well-being, or lack thereof, in ministry. Take time to listen and imagine. How does Jesus respond to you? What words of counsel does he share? Take time to listen to Jesus's words.

In the wake of your sharing, imagine Jesus inviting you to go on a retreat to a deserted place with him. Where does Jesus take you? Visualize this place of retreat. Imagine Jesus nourishing you spiritually, emotionally, physically, or relationally. Does Jesus cook a meal for you? If so, what kind of meal does he prepare? How do you feel after your time in retreat with Jesus?

Be sure to image your leave-taking with Jesus. As you set off down the road toward your regular ministerial duties once more, you discover that a crowd is waiting for you along the way. Visualize the specific people and tasks that await you upon return. Visualize yourself sharing the nourishment Jesus has given you with those people in your congregation and personal life who await your return. With Jesus as your companion, pause a moment to experience the people who are awaiting you with the spirit of compassion and care that you have just received from Jesus.

As you visualize yourself returning to congregational life, take a moment to thank God for those to whom you minister for their trust in you as their pastor. As you conclude this time of prayer, take a few moments to notice your insights and write them in your journal or creative writing notebook.

Sunday Morning Retreats

Although the congregation the two of us copastor worships on Saturday evenings, we recognize that the norm for worship is still Sunday morning. Nevertheless, our suggestions apply whether your congregation worships on Sunday mornings, Saturday nights, or at other times throughout the week. Although it takes great intentionality, we believe that as a pastor you along with your congregants can experience God's presence in worship.

Many pastors lament that Sunday morning is the least worshipful time of the week. Listen to the words of Susan, a Presbyterian pastor in a small Maryland town: "On Sunday mornings, I go from crisis to crisis. Sure, they're all small crises—such as a mess in the bathroom or an absent church school teacher or someone complaining about the details of a church program. But by the time I begin worship, I feel more like a harried businesswoman than a spiritual leader." Steve, a northern Virginia United Methodist pastor, agrees: "In the few minutes I walk from my study to the sanctuary, I am confronted by half a dozen 'urgent' requests to make announcements, one or two logistical questions, and at least one parishioner with a pastoral need to 'see me' after worship."

While compassionate responsiveness to congregants is essential to pastoral ministry, even prior to worship, it is equally essential that we pastors protect the quality of our spiritual lives as we prepare for worship leadership and preaching. We must find creative and compassionate ways to foster contemplation amid the chaos of Sunday morning. The simple fact is that a pastor cannot nurture her or his own sense of worship alone; we need the support and understanding of a congregation. Without coaching on the subject and intentional boundary drawing by you, as a pastor, few congregants recognize how important the quality of a pastor's spiritual life is to her or his congregational leadership, most especially in minutes before worship. Accordingly, we suggest the following Sunday morning practices as ways of tending the holy in preparation for preaching and leading worship.

First, we suggest that pastors finish preparing and practicing their sermons and public prayers at least a day in advance of worship. Ideally, the few hours before worship, whether Saturday night or Sunday morning, should be a time of prayerful contemplation that can flow into your public proclamation and worship leadership. We believe that you should rise early on Sunday morning, making every effort to take time for your regular spiritual and exercise practices as well as your normal eating habits before going to church. As one pastor notes, "My Sundays were out of control until I began a discipline of centering using the Book of Common Prayer, a few minutes of quiet meditation, and a brief walk through my neighborhood. I also make a commitment to spend a few minutes with my wife before I dress for church, and Sunday is the one day of the week that I don't nag at the kids about getting ready. My wife gracefully takes on that chore so that I can remain at peace throughout the morning." To be clear, this male pastor prepares his children's breakfast and helps them get ready for school on a regular basis throughout the week. In our household, Bruce often fixes a Saturday afternoon snack before we leave for our 6:00 PM worship service. Kate notes that "I am usually a last-minute person, and I readily admit that until Bruce and I co-pastored our 'emerging' church with Saturday evening worship, the discipline of spiritual preparation was difficult for me." Our drive to church is often a time for gentle centering and listening to inspirational music on the public radio station as a way of nurturing a sense of contemplative presence in preparation for worship.

Second, even if you are teaching a Sunday school class prior to worship, we suggest that you take a few moments to retreat to your study for a time of prayer and final sermon and liturgical centering. How would your congregants respond if you placed a sign on your study door such as "Please do not disturb—pastor at prayer!" If it would really bother them, you have your work cut out for you.

Third, we encourage you to educate your congregation about the importance of making the time that surrounds worship an opportunity for prayer, praise, and gratitude for everyone in the congregation, not just the pastor. It helps when laypeople take responsibility for gathering announcements before worship so that you can focus prayerfully for the service. Designating hospitality persons who can respond to minor building and personnel emergencies on Sunday mornings is also helpful. By intentionally protecting yourself from a multitude of details, you can enhance your spiritual life and your ability to lead worship and preach with insight and inspiration. Your own attentiveness to your spiritual life prior to worship creates a climate of prayerfulness that radiates throughout the congregation.

Reminding congregants of the vocational interdependence of the body of Christ will transform Sunday mornings from a time of chaotic business to a season of heartfelt praise, prayer, and action. Pastors and congregants alike will truly discover the presence of God in preaching and worship.

In this chapter, we have reflected on how pastors can practice God's presence in the communal acts of ministry—preaching, worship leadership, and teaching—through a commitment to attentiveness to God in both private preparation and public presentation. In the next two chapters, we will focus on the one-to-one aspects of ministry—spiritual formation and pastoral care—in which pastors are called to attend to God's presence in the personal and spiritual journeys of their congregants.

It's a Gift to Be Simple

THE GENTLE ART OF SPIRITUAL GUIDANCE

It has become common for religious seekers of all ages to make the following statement: "I'm spiritual, but not religious." Often this assertion is given as explanation for leaving a particular church or choosing not to attend church at all. Sadly, contemporary Christianity has often failed to address the spiritual hungers of church members and seekers exploring the spiritual resources available beyond the doors of the church. This neglect has spawned a generation of what Kent Ira Groff calls "spiritual orphans," people who have little or no knowledge or attachment to traditional religious institutions.[1]

In the quest to experience the divine, many postmodern seekers believe that the *least* likely place to find spiritual wisdom is in the church. Many seekers believe they can find better spiritual nurture by watching *Oprah*; reading books such as Rhonda Byrne's *The Secret*, Eckhart Tolle's *The Power of Now*, or William Young's *The Shack*; or going on a yoga retreat than by participating with any intentionality in ongoing communal activities such as worship services, Bible studies, or adult educational or service programs. We regretfully admit that in addressing the spiritual journeys of millions of North American seekers, the church has been, to paraphrase the words of Martin Luther King Jr., a "taillight" rather than a "headlight" in illuminating the pathway to spiritual vitality and wholeness for our time.[2] The church has often given people shallow theology and repetitive tasks without providing relevant pathways to experiencing God in and through our particular era's global and personal challenges.

While the two of us recognize that the church's failure to address the spiritual hungers of many contemporary seekers, including youth and young adults within congregations, is the result of many factors, we also believe that our society's emphasis on individualistic rather than communal paths to redemption and fulfillment is no small influence. This, in combination with a basic lack of theological sophistication and depth among laypeople, due in large measure to the inadequacies of Christian education within churches and the church's failure to provide practical spiritual practices, makes a compelling case for lively and mature ministerial spiritual formation. Solid ministerial spiritual formation is necessary if pastors are to respond creatively to the pressing needs of seekers as well as congregational members. If we pastors are not people of prayer and spiritual depth, it is unlikely that we will be able to provide adequate spiritual nurture for congregants, most especially those young seekers and committed Christians who crave an experience and relationship with the divine.

In our reflections on spiritual guidance as one of the essential acts of ministry, we want, first of all, to reaffirm that *every* act of ministry, whether it involves pastoral care, preaching, administration, or social action, reflects the pastor's spiritual life. Whether or not we pastors are consciously aware of it, we are constantly guiding our congregations' spiritual life. Therefore, the two of us believe that the quality of your spiritual life is of utmost importance not only for your own ministerial vitality and pastoral leadership but also for the spiritual well-being of your congregation.

That being said, we must still admit that nurturing a lively and growing spiritual life is just as difficult for us pastors as it is for our congregants. Listen to the stories of faithful pastors, seeking to embody God's vision in their congregational leadership.

Cynthia, a United Church of Christ pastor in Pennsylvania and in midlife, notes that "when I experienced the call to ministry, Jesus was real to me. In the words of the hymn, 'He walked with me and talked with me and told me I was his own.' My prayer life was vital and disciplined. But when I entered seminary, I slowly began to lose the glow that brought me to ministry. My course work caused me to focus on the head and not the heart, and I found my prayer time crowded out by my efforts to balance study, field education, family life, and involvement in my local church. My emphasis on becoming a good minister who could preach a good sermon, wisely choose curricula, and lead effective meetings replaced my initial experience of call to be a spiritual leader and pastoral caregiver. After ten years in ministry, I still find it difficult to make time for daily prayer and devotional reading."

A thirtysomething United Methodist pastor of a suburban Maryland congregation notes with regret that "my seminary rewarded research and writing, but not prayer and meditation. Now that I pastor a church, prayer time is even more difficult to find as I go from meeting to meeting and coordinate the church's capital campaign and building projects. Once again, I'm rewarded for action and accomplishment and not relationship with God."

An evangelical pastor in northern Virginia makes a similar confession, "At the end of the day, I'm the one who's dropped the ball on my spiritual life. I've let the church squeeze me into its image of ministry rather than following God's image of my ministry. Sure, our church is growing and people regularly compliment my preaching, but I have to struggle every day to keep my eyes on Jesus. I feel like Peter, constantly sinking in the stormy seas of ministry, trusting my own efforts rather than God's grace."

In our conversations with seminarians and new pastors over the past several years, the two of us have found that virtually every one of them has entered seminary and continued in ministry because of one specific life-changing spiritual experience or a constellation of events leading them toward seminary and ordained ministry. Whether their experience of call involved hearing God's voice saying, "I have called you to be my servant," as one Presbyterian pastor noted, or a quiet passion over the years that burst forth into a sense of confidence expressed by a Disciples of Christ pastor that "I could only find fulfillment as a congregational pastor," most pastors entered ministry intending to grow in the Spirit and help others experience a similar sense of spiritual intimacy.

Yet, like Martha of Bethany, these pastors have found themselves anxious about many things and often neglectful of the one thing needful for faithful spiritual leadership: an intimate relationship with God, grounded in a life of prayer. Some are stunned and then inspired to deepen their spiritual lives when a friend or spouse challenges them with an observation like the one reported by a United Church of Christ pastor: "I thought it was strange that you could be the spiritual leader of a church when you don't pray much yourself!"

The two of us believe that we pastors are called to be spirit persons whose own familiarity with the divine enables us to help others discover God's presence in the ordinary tasks of their lives as well as God's sustaining care and inspiration in their moments of crisis and challenge.[3] Called to be spiritual guides for others, we pastors must cultivate our awareness of God by learning to "pray without ceasing" throughout the many tasks of ministry (1 Thess. 5:17). In so doing, we will avoid the spiritual dryness confessed in the Song of Solomon: "They made me keeper of the vineyards, but my own vineyard I have not kept!" (1:6) While, as Gerald May notes, the "dark night of the soul" can enter the lives of the most dedicated spiritual leaders, those pastors who continue to nurture their own spiritual formation will still have enough in their spiritual reservoir to respond to their congregations' spiritual needs, even during their dry periods.[4]

The Pastor as Spiritual Guide

Spiritual guidance is the most ubiquitous and difficult to define aspect of congregational ministry. Eugene Peterson suggests that the importance of spiritual guidance is often underestimated because it pertains, by definition, to the private and unseen vocation of the pastor—the life of prayer, devotional reading, and openness to the Spirit of God.[5] In this spirit, we would do well to listen to a variety of approaches to spiritual guidance given by several renowned spiritual directors. According to British spiritual director and pioneer in the revival of spiritual direction among Anglicans, Kenneth Leach, the spiritual director must be a person "of prayer, considering only the glory of God and the good of souls."[6] Tilden Edwards, one of the founders of the Shalem Institute for Spiritual Formation in Bethesda, Maryland, where the two of us took classes in spiritual formation in the 1980s and 1990s, asserts that a spiritual director is "a companion along the pilgrim's way, wanting to be directly open along with the directee to the Spirit—to the undercurrents flowing through the happenings of the directee's life." Edwards continues, "in spiritual direction the focus is on that divine force, on God, as the integral core of our being and purpose." People seek spiritual guidance from pastors and spiritual directors because they want to become "more attuned to God's spirit in our spirit and freely live out of that divine love."[7] Edwards's colleague at the Shalem Institute psychiatrist Gerald May describes the essence of spiritual guidance or direction as a process in which "one person helps another to see or respond to spiritual truth." If spiritual guidance involves, as May suggests, "help, assistance, attention, or facilitation in the process of spiritual formation,"[8] then virtually everything a pastor does is a form of spiritual nurture and guidance.

Practicing the presence of God, while providing spiritual direction to others, involves ongoing nurture of one's awareness of God's many voices and movements within our own lives as well as the lives of seekers and congregants with whom we are called to minister. If we affirm that God is present as a gentle, guiding presence in each moment of our experience and in every personal encounter, then the goal of spiritual guidance is to help people experience God moment by moment and day by day. Our primary spiritual task is to help people discover God's many possibilities for their lives, given their unique gifts, personal characteristics, and relational and occupational context. Spiritual guidance in the practice of ministry is not so much a well-defined practice but an all-pervasive way of life in which we pray constantly throughout the day. Spiritual care is not one more thing to learn but a way of experiencing the world so that each moment reflects the interplay of God's call and our human response. While our technical skills and expertise can, for a time, mask an undisciplined prayer life, eventually our lack of spiritual depth will be reflected in diminishing the quality of our preaching, administration, and pastoral care. As the two of us reflect on the importance of spiritual practices in faithful ministry, we believe that at the heart of vital and transforming spiritual guidance are the twin foci of *simplicity of the spirit* and *constancy in awareness of God's presence.*

The Pathway of Simplicity

If we assume that one of primary roles of ministry is to be a spirit person or spiritual guide, then today's pastors are the spiritual children of the shamans, magi, medicine people, and male and female sages of the Hebraic tradition. As stated earlier, most pastors, like their spiritual parents, entered the pathway of ministry as a result of gradual or dramatic spiritual experiences that transformed their way of experiencing themselves and the world. Even those pastors who struggled for years with their sense of call before entering seminary experienced, for the most part, a God-ward pull that drew them toward holy things and holy persons. Like their spiritual predecessors, they could not fully experience personal wholeness or fulfillment until they embodied this holy call in the everyday ministerial tasks of teaching, healing, comforting, and providing guidance for the grieving and dying.

In claiming their historic and contemporary vocation, pastors are called to be people who have experienced the holy and show others, by their lives and ministries, how to experience holiness in their own lives. While the two of us affirm the ministry of the laity and priesthood of all believers, we also affirm that pastors *are called* to embody the invitation to experience God's vital presence within their congregations. Separated from an ongoing experience of God's presence in the complexities of daily life, pastors become little more than technicians who know the right gestures and actions but who are unable to awaken others to the God in whom "we live and move and have our being" (Acts 17:28). In the pluralistic, high-tech postmodern world in which we live, seekers and congregants alike yearn for spiritual leaders who not only believe something but also have an ongoing experience of the holy that inspires them to share the good news with others by deed and inspiration and by doctrine and words. In a world of complexity, people yearn for the simple gift of experiencing God in all things, from checking their e-mail to multitasking at both home and the office.

Jesus called his first followers to the pathway of simplicity in their own time that still resonates for those who seek to find wholeness in their daily tasks. He invited them to move from anxiety about many things to experiencing peace in all things by following the one God in the many adventures of life. To harried followers then and now, Jesus suggested an alternative way of life, grounded in trusting God's presence and seeking God's realm in every situation. Take a moment to listen prayerfully to Jesus's pathway of simplicity as if it is addressed to you in your pastoral busyness. In fact, these words *are* addressed to you in your life and ministry:

Therefore I tell you, do not worry about your life, what you shall eat
or what you shall drink, or about your body, what you will wear. Is
not life more than food, and the body more than clothing? Look at
the birds of the air; they neither sow nor reap nor gather into barns,
and yet your [Divine Parent] feeds them. . . . Consider the lilies of
the field, how they grow; they neither toil nor spin, yet I tell you,
even Solomon in all of his glory was not clothed like one of these.
. . . Your [Divine Parent] knows that you need all these things. But
strive first for the kingdom of God and [God's] righteousness, and
all these things will be given to you as well.

So do not worry about tomorrow, for tomorrow will bring
worries of its own. Today's trouble is enough for today (Matt.
6:25–26, 28–29, 33–34).

Once, in an exercise in *lectio divina* with a group of pastors
from Maryland and Pennsylvania, a number of the pastors
experienced these words as an invitation to see their ministry
from a new perspective. "I always seem to be on the go," one
pastor confessed. "I think that my congregation's growth and
the quality of its programs are entirely in my hands. Sometimes
I stay awake at night worrying about a meeting that hasn't even
been scheduled. But where's the grace in all of this hurry? I
need to stop and listen to what God has to say to me today!"
Another responded, "The word that struck me was 'Strive first
for God's kingdom.' It's not about my vision alone, but God's
vision for my ministry and this church. I need to listen more
and talk less. I need to let go of my plans or be willing to be
flexible, so I can attend to God's plans." A third pastor noted,
"This is all about beauty. Can my ministry be beautiful? Can
I see the presence of God in birds and flowers, and help my
congregation to experience God's beauty, too? Sometimes we
are so busy at church trying to save the world that we don't even
notice its beauty. Maybe I need to go on a retreat in the woods
and just simply *be*, before I try to share any wisdom with my
congregation."

To seek God's kingdom is to be attentive God's "words" of love and beauty in the many diverse voices of human life and nature. The path of simplicity calls pastors to *pause* and *notice* the places where God is present in everyday encounters that define the practice of ministry as well as *pause* and *notice* God's wisdom in the nonhuman world of sunsets, scudding clouds, migrating geese, and verdant fields. God's presence in all things calls us to simplicity amid diversity, awareness of the lively presence on the one intimate and creative reality within the many changing moments of our personal and professional lives. This one reality comes to us under many guises and many vocational callings.

Take a moment to reflect on your experience of God in the many events of your life. What is the one thing you are called to do in your current professional setting? Where do you experience God's passion igniting your own passion in life and ministry? What is your mission that enables you to discern the difference between the wheat and the chaff of ministry and those activities that bring health or disease to your life and the life of your congregation?

Knowing God's callings within our many callings enables us to practice faithful and effective ministry. While ministry at its best is flexible and agile in responding to unexpected events, pastors who know their unique and evolving mission as spirit persons can navigate gracefully, creatively, and calmly the constantly changing vocations of ministry. Jesus's own sense of vocation enabled him to follow his calling despite his followers' demands on his time and expectations of his ministry. When Peter and his companions interrupt Jesus's prayer time with the crisis of the moment, Jesus tells them he must listen first to God's vision for his life and follow his mission to the wider world as God's healer and teacher, "For that is what I came out to do" (Mark 1:38).

The Gospel stories describe Jesus as a person with a clear but flexible and constantly evolving sense of mission to follow the Spirit in preaching the good news of God's reign by healing the sick, welcoming the lost, embracing the outcast, and inspiring people to embody the abundant life God intends for them. Jesus's simplicity of focus enabled him to reach out to the world in all its messy complexity.

Simplicity of life involves ongoing attentiveness to God's vision in each moment. The two of us have been influenced by the Russian Orthodox classic *The Way of a Pilgrim*, which describes the spiritual journey of a nineteenth-century seeker. Inspired by Paul's admonition to "pray without ceasing" (1 Thess. 5:17), the pilgrim centers his life around an ancient prayer—"Lord Jesus Christ, have mercy upon me, a sinner"—until the Jesus Prayer becomes the melody of his life, guiding his responses to synchronous encounters along his pilgrim way.[9]

What would it mean for you as a pastor to pray constantly throughout the many events of your life? What would it be like for your prayers to be as near to you as your breathing? What would it mean for you to recognize, in the spirit of the plaque on Carl Jung's study door, that "bidden or unbidden, God is here?"

Stephanie, a Disciples of Christ pastor in Virginia, breathes a quiet "Lord, have mercy" whenever the phone rings or she hears a knock on her study door. A United Methodist pastor, Charles keeps his spiritual center by humming his favorite hymns throughout the day. Charles notes, "I have hymns that I repeat day after day, like 'Be Still My Soul' or 'Great Is Thy Faithfulness,' but I also break out in song when I am feeling joyful or when I anticipate trouble in my parish. Sometimes the next hymn I sing is as surprising to me as it is to my secretary or to my wife. But singing that hymn always gives me what I need in the moment. Without a song in my heart and on my lips, I'd be lost." In the spirit of today's global spirituality, Cathy, a Unitarian Universalist minister from Massachusetts, practices Thich Nhat Hanh's "walking prayers" as she chants breath by breath and step by step throughout the day, "Breathing in, I calm my body, breathing out, I smile."[10]

In *The Four Seasons of Ministry*, the two of us shared a simple breath prayer that Kate learned as a college student in Claremont, California. "I breathe the spirit deeply in, and blow it joyfully [or any other feeling you want to lift up to God] out again."[11] To this day, Kate uses this prayer regularly as a way to help her pause and notice her deepest feelings, including the quality of her physical well-being, and then spiritually open and yield to divine healing. In his quest for illumination, Bruce has a simple phrase he employs whenever he goes from one task to another, encounters someone in the seminary hallway or at church, or picks up the phone. Inhaling, he says silently "God's" and exhaling he says silently, "light."

Simplicity is the heart of what Gerald May described in terms of *pausing, noticing, opening,* and *yielding and stretching* to the many voices of God emerging in and through each moment of experience and encounter. While we can seldom fully discern God's voice, we can honestly experience and probe feeling tones that guide us toward beauty, truth, reconciliation, attentiveness, and love. Simplicity grounds us in the holy here and the holy now of God's lively presence in all things. It leads to the gift of awareness and attention, necessary for experiencing God's holiness in ourselves and in the life of another.

The Pathway of Awareness

Prior to the advent of technological medicine, physicians and nurses spent more time observing and touching the patient than examining medical charts in their quest for a medical diagnosis. While the two of us affirm, and have benefited from, the growing use of technology in both diagnosis and treatment, we recognize the importance of the senses of touch, sight, hearing, taste, and smell, still emphasized by complementary health caregivers, chiropractors, and physicians trained outside of the United States, in truly getting to know both the patient's condition and the appropriate healing response. In so doing, healing professionals become more deeply attuned to the rhythm of health and illness among their patients. Medical researchers, such as Candace Pert, explore what is now being described as the neurobiology of touch that connects health care professionals emotionally and spiritually with their patients.[12]

Spiritual leadership, in its ability to heal personal and communal brokenness, has often been compared to medicine. In fact, the earliest spiritual guides united the practices of law, medicine, and priesthood in their quest to align or restore the relationship between the divine and human individuals and communities. Jesus is described as the great physician as a result of his care for the whole person—mind, body, and spirit.

Today's spiritual guides bear the legacy of Jesus's healing ministry as well as the healing gifts of earlier physicians of the spirit. Like the healer Jesus, these spiritual guides knew that spiritual healing comes from asking wise questions, and, then, patiently listening to the words of their spiritual companions, and from simple acts of hospitality and theological teaching. They recognized that in order for our theological beliefs to be life transforming, they needed to be embodied and experienced in companionship through the ordinary and repeated rituals of everyday life.

The pathways of simplicity and awareness in our spiritual companionship with others complement one another in the vocation of ministry. The *path of simplicity* involves the quest for inner integrity, including a holistic sense of our emotional lives in all their complexity, and an awareness of God's presence in the minister's personal and professional life. The *path of awareness* focuses on taking time to experience God's presence in the subtleties of the lives of those to whom we are called to minister, whether in one-on-one spiritual direction, group spiritual direction, worship, Christian education, administration, pastoral care, or youth ministry. Spiritual guidance is grounded in an ongoing commitment to experiencing One Life moving in many ways through the multiplicity of our individual and collective adventures. It involves the awareness of God's movements in the lives of others and our commitment to being companions to others in ways that help them experience God in their everyday lives and vocational decision making. As we pastors seek to provide spiritual direction for congregants, we must be open to the undercurrents of the Spirit in another person's life and in our own lives.[13] Our exploration of God's presence in the complexities of our own lives enables us to experience God in the many-faceted experiences of those to whom we minister. This obviously includes our own struggles to be faithful to God in the full spectrum of our experience, including experiences of pain, anger, doubt, trauma, and guilt.

Margaret Guenther captures the intersection of the pathways of simplicity and awareness in the spiritual care of people and congregations with her counsel that spiritual guides must attend first to their own housekeeping by creating their own inner order. So, too, we pastors must take time for our own spiritual housekeeping so that we can provide a hospitable space for others to grow.[14] Daily disciplines of inner housekeeping allow us to live by *kairos*, God's abundant time, even when we must work in accordance with schedules that require moving from task to task throughout the day. By attending to the holiness of time and space in our own lives, we may provide the greatest possible gift to another person in her or his otherwise hurried lifestyle: that is, the gift of leisure and refreshment. As Guenther suggests, our own sense of spaciousness enables the directee to experience her or his own life as unhurried and spacious. In the spacious interplay of call and response that characterizes wise spiritual care, we as pastors and those for whom we are spiritual companions can both experience and celebrate God's everlasting now.

In his text on desert spirituality, Thomas Merton describes the final counsel of a North African spiritual guide: "'The monk should be all eye, like the cherubim and seraphim.'"[15] This same counsel is appropriate for we who seek to embody what author

John Yungblut describes as the "gentle art of spiritual guidance" in our pastoral work and spiritual care.[16] Indeed, awareness of God's presence in others' lives is the practical pastoral response to the Christian doctrine of omnipresence. When we recognize God present everywhere, including *here* in our own life and also in the life of the one who sits beside us, we can open our lives and ministries to a sense of holy adventure in which God constantly speaks to and through us in commonplace and dramatic moments.

Gerald May notes the intimate relationship between our own spiritual awareness and our ability to support the spiritual adventures of others. According to May, our primary task in spiritual care situations is "to encourage within ourselves the moment-by-moment attention towards God as frequently as possible during spiritual direction sessions."[17] This can only occur if we, like the anonymous author of *The Way of the Pilgrim*, make the constant awareness of God a practiced priority. Like any other habit, we cannot conjure spiritual attentiveness for an hour-long session with a congregant if we do not regularly spend time caring for our own spiritual growth through the practices of prayer and contemplation and ongoing conversations with our own spiritual director. Through intentionally opening to the gracefulness of each moment, whether in joy or sorrow, we can best enable others to experience God in their struggles and seeking, and grief and celebration.

The *cultivation of leisure and awareness* in relationship to oneself and others is essential to spiritual attentiveness. Even if we have only a few quiet moments in a day of many appointments, one holy moment spent in attunement with God, oneself, and another can awaken them, and ourselves, to God's infinite and abiding grace in amazing ways.

Whenever she has a spiritual direction appointment with a congregant, Kate prepares herself by deepening and slowing down her breath as she walks around the lower level study and office we have created for spiritual direction and Reiki treatments and classes. She seeks to create a hospitable and aesthetic space by dimming the lights and lighting incense. While she waits for her directee to arrive, she takes a few moments to center herself in God's ambient and intimate presence. When her directee arrives, she lights a central candle as reminder that God is enlightening both pastor and congregant.

Bruce often invites seminary students who seek his counsel to take a walk through the grounds of Franklin and Marshall College, adjacent to the seminary, as they talk. As a follower of Augustine's maxim, *solvitur ambulando*, "It is solved in the walking," Bruce believes that walking outside clears his mind and opens his companion and himself to new and creative ways to look at God's presence in their lives. Even in our marriage, we have discovered that walking and talking together awakens us to new horizons of intimacy and creativity as a couple. Open spaces serve to open our hearts and minds to new possibilities for partnership and love in our marriage.

The practice of sharing a spiritual adventure with another in one-on-one spiritual care is an act of deep listening and profound awareness, which is best grounded in disciplined attentiveness and prayer. As we listen to the spiritual journeys of others, we are challenged to attend to our own moment-by-moment spiritual awareness. Gerald May suggests that we develop the habit, during our encounters with people who seek our spiritual guidance, of asking ourselves questions such as the following: Am I, the pastor or director, attentive to God in this moment? What is this person's spiritual concern? What is getting in the way of her experiencing the holy?[18] Asking these questions of ourselves keeps us "in the room" and present to God's presence in the moment, whether in one-on-one spiritual care or with a small group. In this holy relational moment, God calls us to be in open to the "sacrament of the present moment" rather than looking toward the next appointment or our plans for the evening. The sacrament of the present moment, as Jean-Pierre de Caussade notes, enables us to discover God in all things and all things in God, beginning with our own spiritually embodied experience and expanding to embrace the embodied spiritual experience of the one to whom I am listening.[19] As Buddhist spiritual guide Thich Nhat Hanh notes, "The miracle is not walking on water. The miracle is to walk on the green earth in the present moment."[20]

In her practice of spiritual direction, Kate finds that the most common hidden impediment to prayer is, in fact, fear. When someone is caught in a fight, flight, or freeze response to a stressful or traumatic situation, one of the most difficult things they can do is to engage the present moment. The first step toward healing of mind, body, and spirit often occurs when we help them, often tearfully, claim their fear along with the angelic reassurance, "Do not be afraid, God is with you" in this safe and healing environment (Luke 1). The simple act of presence ministry by a sensitive and trustworthy pastor can be the first step in transforming fear into trust, and opening the doors to loving God and other people.

While most congregational ministers spend only a handful of hours a month in planned spiritual direction with congregants, much of their most significant spiritual care comes unexpectedly and synchronously. Bruce recalls such a sacred conversation occurring when a first-year seminarian knocked on his study door at Lancaster Theological Seminary. Like so many other seekers, she began her visit with the words, "I know you're very busy, but . . ." As is his practice when someone enters his study, Bruce invited her to sit in one of the wing chairs as he logged off his computer, stepped out from behind his desk, and sat across from her. In the next half hour, she shared the liveliness of her call and yet her uncertainty about the traditional doctrines of the church. Bruce soon realized that he was on holy ground. He quietly took a breath and gave thanks for the opportunity to share in her quest to join experience, vocation, and belief. At that moment, Bruce knew that his task was twofold: first, to listen deeply and, second, to ask questions based on what she shared verbally and emotionally in order to help her discern the movements of divine wisdom in her life. The questions he asked involved her experience of call, spiritual practices, and current sense of God's presence in her life.

In that first meeting, whenever he was tempted to "give her the answers she needed," Bruce took a breath and reminded himself that if she were attentive, God would give her the answers and that his task at this moment was to provide a safe, graceful, spacious, and accepting space for her exploration into the holy. During the next few months, Bruce met regularly with this seminarian over coffee in a set of Adirondack chairs at Franklin and Marshall College across the street from his study or on walks in the neighborhood adjoining the seminary. While Bruce takes little credit for the path to faithful ministry this young pastor has taken, he rejoices when she updates him regularly about her adventures in congregational ministry. This young woman has found a place for herself denominationally and has found her way to a sense of theological and vocational clarity. In retrospect, Bruce recognizes that a several-month journey that eventuated in a seminarian clarifying her sense of call and pastoral identity began with an unexpected knock on the door and a few minutes of caring, open, and prayerful attention.

In the course of this and many other unexpected spiritual encounters, Bruce uses the movement from his desk to the wing chair as both a symbolic gesture and spiritual practice that reminds him and his companion that we all sit together as seekers in God's presence. In spiritual direction, there is no ultimate separation between minister and congregant. Both of us are in need of God's inspiration and guidance on our pilgrim way. The few seconds Bruce takes to move to his wing chair allows him to breathe deeply, centering himself and his companion in God's dynamic and life-transforming presence.

Spiritual care can and should involve children as well as senior adults. In his work as interim pastor at a United Church of Christ congregation near Hagerstown, Maryland, Bruce recalls noticing a fifth grader who always read during the worship service. She was without a doubt the brightest child in the congregation. One Sunday during the coffee hour, Bruce asked her what she was reading. Surprised that an adult, most especially the minister, would be interested, she blushed and said, "*Harry Potter*." At that moment Bruce knew that he needed to begin to read the Harry Potter series himself. For the next several months, Bruce spent a few minutes asking her questions and listening to the joyfulness in her answers. Bruce reminded her that she could also be a heroic person, a Harry Potter or Hermione in her own life. Today she is an honor student on the verge of entering college and their Harry Potter bond remains.

In another encounter, this time during a baptismal class, Bruce asked a sixth grade Disciples of Christ baptizand about what she found interesting at school. Her initial response, "I'm not very smart. I don't do well in school," gave him pause. Over the next few weeks, he took a few moments each week to ask about her studies, to listen to her issues of self-affirmation, and then to remind her, with all honesty, that she was "smarter than she thought." The next semester she received all Bs, and today she is in community college in the Hagerstown area and credits Bruce with helping her build her self-confidence. Kate has enjoyed her extended spiritual reflection times with young children during children's sermons and coffee hour, focusing on the *Star Wars* sagas, Pokemon cards, and Transformer action figures.

While some people might ask if any of these encounters constituted spiritual care, the two of us respond with a whole-hearted yes! We believe that a dynamic and holistic understanding of spiritual care enables us to see all encounters as holy encounters. The two of us see God's hand in transforming minds, bodies, spirits, and emotions through a wide variety of media and literature. God is just as concerned about the unfolding of a child's life and her developing a sense of connection to faithful realities beyond herself as the discernment process of a recent college graduate or adult in midlife considering retirement. Such holy transformations can occur as the result of a few minutes' attentiveness and well-chosen word of guidance or encouragement.

During his eighteen months as interim minister of a Disciples of Christ congregation in western Maryland, Bruce experienced the "gentle art of spiritual direction" in the companionship of pastoral calls and strategic visioning with the congregation's board chair. As they drove through the hilly countryside of western Maryland, Bruce and his congregant reflected together on such wide-ranging topics as cosmology, the problem of evil, sin, and the second coming of Jesus. Bruce soon realized that these conversations were more than just academic or administrative in nature; they reflected his congregant's concern for the meaning of his life, his uncertainty about the afterlife, and his need to experience grace as he looked back on his life. Bruce's conversation partner had been theologically starved by a long-term pastor who discouraged any deviation from his conservative faith position. As his assumptions about what was going on shifted, Bruce needed to pause, notice, and open to his companion's questions and, more important, the questions behind the questions. Rather than filling the conversation with "right" theological answers, he needed to pause so that his companion's sense of God's presence would gracefully emerge on God's gentle terms rather than Bruce's own agenda. He needed to trust that in their conversations, his companion would experience guidance and grace.

The spiritually concerned pastor is "all eyes and ears," as she opens to experiencing God in every formal and informal pastoral encounter. We two have found that in order to respond to congregants' spiritual needs, we need to immerse ourselves in the long tradition of Christian spiritual direction and mystical experience and in contemporary and postmodern voices of spiritual transformation. Above all, we need to be the incarnation of graceful care and spiritual affirmation by caring for our own spiritual lives as much as we care for the spiritual lives of others. Along with daily prayer, contemplation, and study, we have found it helpful to participate in group or one-on-one spiritual direction or find a colleague who can be our *anam cara*, or friend of the soul. We need people who mirror God's presence in our lives as we mirror God's presence in the lives of those to whom we are called to pastor.

Kate sees her regular appointments with her own spiritual director as an essential aspect of her own practice as a pastor and spiritual director. Over the years, her spiritual directors have been wisdom givers who created space for Kate to slow down and take time to explore her life's challenges and concerns from a variety of perspectives and, then, to discover which perspective was most authentically her own. Several of her spiritual directors have been artists as well as spiritual guides. They have shared with Kate the value of artistically expressing her spiritual discernment through music and the visual arts. Inspired by her own experiences in spiritual direction, Kate often incorporates work with the visual arts into her own practice as a spiritual director.

Finding your own appropriate spiritual discipline enables you to create a space in which life-transforming experiences of God's presence can emerge. In your commitment to experience holiness everywhere, you can become a spiritual midwife of sorts, following God's guidance in bringing forth the spiritual gifts of those you meet. Like Quaker mystic George Fox, we are called to go "cheerfully over the face of the earth, answering to that of God in everyone."[21]

Practicing the Presence of God in Spiritual Guidance

How can you as a pastor seeking to be a spiritual guide for others become "all eyes and ears" in your awareness of the subtle as well as the obvious presence of God in the lives of those to whom you are called to minister? We believe that divine guidance comes to us through all the senses as well as through insights, intuitions, visions, and dreams. From this perspective, practicing the presence of God in spiritual guidance is not about any sort of ascetic, life-denying discipline but simply involves awakening to holy moments in your own life as the foundation for your ability to discern such moments in the lives of others. We have found that the practices of (1) creative spiritual autobiography, (2) praying the moments, and (3) experiencing God in interruptions are particularly helpful ways to deepen moment-by-moment experiences of God's presence in our personal and professional encounters.

Creative Spiritual Autobiography

If we regard our lives as a holy adventure in which God is present every step of the way, then we can begin to heighten our awareness of the holiness of our lives and the lives of others by remembering moments in which we have experienced God's presence. In this section, the two of us elaborate on, from a slightly different angle, our previous comments on the importance of spiritual autobiography in practicing the presence of God in preaching. We will suggest two simple ways to heighten and deepen your awareness of God in the present moment and in your life as a whole: drawing your spiritual adventure and remembering your call.

DRAWING YOUR SPIRITUAL ADVENTURE

First, we invite you to chart your spiritual adventure from childhood to the present time, using colors and symbols as you deem appropriate. What would it look like for you to create such colorful timeline? You may do this in one hour-long setting or over an extended period of time. Take a few moments to reflect on a moment of your childhood, pondering when you first experienced the reality of God in your life. Then, move slowly forward through the stages of your life from elementary school to high school, college, seminary, and adult life, noting God moments as well as the overall feeling tone of each season. What feelings did these experiences elicit in you? What color and symbol would represent these experiences? When you reach the present time, pause a moment to give thanks for God's guiding presence in your life.

If you have chosen to draw a timeline or spiral to describe the unfolding of your spiritual life, you may have highlighted certain God moments as well as moments of spiritual dryness or seasons of darkness. As you conclude, take some time to see your life as a whole, and reflect upon any patterns of grace and inspiration, call and response, in your spiritual adventure.

REMEMBERING YOUR CALL

In the tradition of Samuel, Esther, Paul, Peter, and Mary the mother of Jesus, most of us took our first steps on the road to seminary and ordained ministry as the result of an experience of divine inspiration or call. When we look back on our initial experiences of God and retell the story of our call to ministry, we find refreshment for living out our vocation in "just such a time as this" (Est. 4:14).

In this exercise, take several minutes to breathe deeply as you open yourself to divine inspiration. In your memory, go back to your first awareness of God's call for you to ordained ministry. You may have noted this awareness in drawing or journaling your spiritual autobiography. If so, what color and symbol did you use to represent that experience? Visualize the time, place, and process of call. Remember how you felt at the time. Now, take a few minutes to visualize the unfolding of your call as it led you to eventually enrolling in seminary. What were your challenges in beginning the path to ministry? What sustained you as you deepened your sense of call?

Now, take a few minutes to reflect on your current sense of call in ministry. Where are you experiencing God's presence to be most vital in your life and ministry today? What is sustaining your sense of call and what is distracting you from your experience of God's call in your life? Prayerfully note what brings a sense of joy and fulfillment. What prevents you from fully embodying your call in ministry? Where do you sense or intuit God's call toward future ministerial and personal adventures? Conclude this exercise by sharing your experiences of distraction, loss, accomplishment, and gratitude with God. You may choose to take some time to journal your experience and to draw a picture or paint a watercolor that depicts your current experience of God's call in your life.

Praying the Moments of Ministry

Our attentiveness to God's movements in others' lives is intimately related to our awareness of God's presence in the moment by moment experiences of our own lives. While we "see in a mirror dimly" (1 Cor. 13:12) drifting from moments of God awareness to God forgetfulness, the two of us believe that God is always moving within the "sighs too deep for words" (Rom. 8:26) that emerge from a person's deepest spiritual identity. We suggest that you pause regularly to listen to God's sighs breathing through your own sighs. Take a moment simply to pause and notice the quality of your breath: Is your breath full and calm or shallow and anxious?

Awareness of God's presence in one's life is more a matter of spiritual intimacy than doctrinal orthodoxy, despite the interdependence of theological visions and spiritual experiences and the importance of theological reflection in sustaining a pastor's vocation. Accordingly, your calling is to practice the presence of God in the many diverse moments of life and ministry.

While there is no *one* way to pray your day-to-day moments of ministry, the two of us believe that the ability to experience the holy results from opening to God's presence through a plethora contemplative prayer and meditation practices that awaken one to God throughout the day. We suggest that pastors experiment with a wide variety of practices of spiritual attentiveness. For example, one pastor prays the Jesus Prayer throughout the day. He silently prays "Lord, have mercy on me" as he walks from the parking lot to the church study, whenever he picks up the phone or logs onto e-mail, and in the midst of meetings when he begins to feel a growing sense of anxiety. He prays the Jesus Prayer before he begins his sermon and during private spiritual guidance sessions. This pastor confesses that "these simple words of prayer keep me on track throughout the day and remind me that my vocation is to share God's grace wherever I am. Sometimes, in the heat of a congregational board meeting, I stop and pray, because then and there I know I really need God's mercy!"

Kate is drawn to simple, wordless prayers, grounded in the affirmation that the Holy Spirit breathes in and through us. Throughout the day, we encourage you to pause a moment to notice your breathing and then take a deep centering breath as a way of connecting with God's Spirit in your life. Such breath prayers remind us that God is with us and those with whom we minister, whether we are involved in giving one-on-one spiritual guidance or trying to finish the church newsletter on time. As a result of taking a seminar on contemplative prayer, a United Methodist pastor in central Pennsylvania now affirms that "peace is only a breath away." Her breath prayer keeps her centered on God's grace rather than the stresses of ministry. "When I breathe with the spirit," she notes, "I know I that am safe and that I can be calm even on the busiest days at church." Kate finds that deep, slow breath prayers energize and open her to God's healing presence in spiritual direction and pastoral care settings.

Often easily distracted by his ruminations on his daily schedule, Steven, a Mennonite pastor in central Pennsylvania,

breathes deeply and regularly in the course of his spiritual care
and counseling appointments in order to stay focused on his
parishioner's needs and not on his next appointment and the
tasks he must complete before he leaves for home. "The simple
act of breath keeps me in sync with God's presence as I listen to the words of my parishioners. When I finally respond
with a comment or a question, it comes from God's deeper wisdom rather than my temptation to problem solve." Steven has
learned that healthy spiritual care involves more breathing and
praying and less talking on his part. "Some of my best sermons
are silent. Sometimes somebody thanks me for my wise advice
when I've said virtually nothing."

Experiencing God in the Interruptions

Bruce notes the irony of feeling annoyed when a student
knocked unexpectedly on the door of his seminary study early
one morning. Although he quickly recovered his equanimity
and was able to respond to the student's personal need, Bruce
felt a wave of embarrassment when he returned to his computer keyboard only to remember that he was writing a sermon
on the hospitality of entertaining angels unaware. Since that
time, Bruce has been committed to experiencing interruptions,
whether in the form of a ringing phone, a knock on his study,
or a request from Kate, as an invitation to prayer. Bruce agrees
with the observation of Shelly, a midcareer Presbyterian pastor: "My life as a mother, daughter, spouse, and pastor is one
long series of interruptions. The only thing I can be sure of
when I go to work each day is that I will be interrupted several
times before the day is through. I keep my sense of calm in
ministry by taking time for a short prayer every fifteen minute
minutes and whenever the phone rings or someone knocks on
my study door. My prayers aren't fancy. I simply ask for God be
with me in this moment or this encounter."

Kate believes that introverts like Bruce and Shelly have an easier time praying the interruptions than more extraverted people. For Kate, and many strong extraverts, praying the interruptions is almost impossible to practice. Kate asserts that "distractions are just distractions!" Like other extraverts, she goes with the flow of distractions, recognizing that the process, including her response to distractions, itself is the reality. There is no failure for those who seek to practice God's presence in ministry. Grace is everything. Each person is called to draw, write, remember, and breathe their own unique spirituality as their gift to God and those with whom they pastor.

Pastoral Care as
Healing Presence

In the most recent presidential election, a political ad featured a late night phone call and the question, Who will answer the phone at three o'clock in the morning? While pastoral emergencies occur at every hour of the day, the two of us must admit that we dread *the phone call*, whether it occurs in the middle of the night, at the beginning of our workday, or during our lunch break.

Kate remembers receiving one such phone call that interrupted an afternoon off many years ago at our home in Potomac, Maryland. She knew something was amiss when she heard the tone of her secretary's voice. In a matter of moments, she had to move from sabbath time to crisis ministry as she received the news that one of the congregation's teenagers, along with a few other teens, had just been killed in an automobile crash involving an out-of-control dump truck. Adrenaline flowing, Kate gathered as much information as she could from her secretary, paused to say a brief prayer, threw on some appropriate pastoral garments, and headed for what she knew would be a heartbreaking encounter with grieving parents. A parent herself, Kate reflected on the feelings of shock, helplessness, grief, and anger that she would have experienced if she had been confronted with similar news.

Within twenty-four hours, Kate found herself performing the multiple tasks associated with any death in the congregation:

comforter and grief counselor, liaison between the parents and
the mortuary, liturgical planner and worship coordinator, hom-
ilist, life chronicler, and communicator of news to the congregation and the wider community. Kate soon discovered that
she needed not only to respond to the pastoral needs of the
grieving family but also to the anguish of the congregation's
and community's teenagers, many of whom had never previously encountered death or been to church, apart from Christ-
mas Eve services. Even though Kate placed the needs of the
grieving family at the forefront of her ministry, she knew that
as solo pastor she could not drop all her other responsibilities
at church. She needed to triage her tasks, taking some time for
Sunday sermon and worship preparation, pastoral phone calls,
and administrative supervision, in the midst of responding to
the many logistical, pastoral, spiritual, and liturgical tasks that
accompany an unexpected and heartbreaking congregational or
community tragedy. In the weeks and months ahead, Kate had
to respond to a family and a congregation in crisis, while insuring that she would attend to the everyday tasks of ministry and
congregational life with faithfulness, grace, and excellence. Kate
recognized that her task was to be a healer who provided space
for people to experience grief along with God's invitation to
wholeness. She was challenged to integrate despair and hope
from the perspective of God's future.

As she looks back on this congregational tragedy and other
times of intense pastoral care giving, Kate recalls that her ability to be present as a spiritual leader, healer, and comforter to
the grief-stricken family, congregation, and community members depended on three things: her ongoing prayer disciplines;
the personal support and professional counsel of colleagues
and family; and a solid lay congregational pastoral care team.
Kate notes, "I was able to be a healing presence during this
time of crisis because of my regular practices of daily prayer,
which gave me strength through familiar mental and spiritual
structures; walks with my husband, Bruce, which grounded me

in my body; and gardening, which grounds and renews within me a sense of faith and hope in God's 'greening' powers in all things. I realized that if I didn't take care of my own emotional and spiritual life, I would be unable to respond with care, sensitivity, and professionalism to the spiritual needs of the family and congregation."

A single parent, Deborah recalls that during her first month as pastor of a United Church of Christ congregation in western Pennsylvania, she performed nine funerals, four of which related to a boating accident. Already weary from moving across country to a new parsonage and getting to know a new congregation, Deborah knew that she soon would be spiritually and relationally depleted if she did not take time for self-care and personal and professional support. She asked her recently retired parents to come visit for two weeks to help her organize the house, cook meals, and care for her ten-year-old son. She also called her regional judicatory official for a referral to a spiritual director who would help her stay "spiritually grounded during this time of congregational crisis and personal stress." In addition, also sought out the spiritual and professional counsel of two experienced women pastors in the neighborhood. Several years later, Deborah is still meets regularly with her spiritual director and has become close friends with the colleagues she initially called upon for nurture and support during this critical time.

Thankfully, the majority of our pastoral care encounters are not matters of life and death, fraught with complex congregational and community dynamics of grief and loss. Most encounters typically relate to ongoing issues of illness, personal growth, relationships, self-discovery, trauma, and bereavement. While these pastoral care issues are not as dramatic as unexpected deaths and diagnoses of life-threatening illness, they require just as much pastoral sensitivity and healing care, because every crisis is unique to those who are in the midst of it. Every crisis is a spiritual emergency in which the care of a sensitive

and professional pastor can make the difference between hope
and hopelessness, courage and cowardice, and responsibility
and helplessness. Indeed, one of our tasks as pastors is to present images of hope and new life to people for whom, at the
moment, the future appears bleak and uncertain.

When Bruce served as Protestant chaplain at Georgetown
University, he met weekly with a first-year student who was not
only facing the challenges of a new environment far away from
home but also dealing with feelings of helplessness surrounding
her mother's recent diagnosis of multiple sclerosis. She wanted
to stay in school, but also was contemplating transferring to a
university closer to home, despite her parents' assurances that
they were doing alright. Each week, Bruce and Diane met for
prayer, conversation, and theological reflection. Bruce saw his
primary vocation in this pastoral encounter as one of listening
to her questions of faith; helping her creatively face her doubts
and anger; providing a secure, faithful, and safe environment
for her to experience her many conflicting feelings; and helping
her reflect theologically on what was happening in her life.

Years later when she was on the verge of graduating, Bruce
was surprised when Diane shared that their afternoons together in her first semester were pivotal in her personal and spiritual growth. As Bruce recalls, "I prepared for each visit by closing
my study door for a few minutes to take time to be still in God's
presence. I realized that God would enable me to listen with
care and speak with wisdom if I first centered myself in a healing presence greater than my own. I realized that I needed to
listen to her experience and, then, respond prayerfully in ways
that would help her find strength to face her challenges." Particularly during congregants' times of crisis, transition, uncertainty, and trauma, we pastors are called to be God's healing
partners, sharing the grace we have received in ways that bring
comfort, transformation, clarity, and wholeness to those whose
lives we touch. Such sensitive pastoral caring is not accidental,

but is the fruit of spiritually grounded disciplines of practicing the presence of God in ministry.

Transforming Vulnerability

The story is told of young Hindu prince who lived a life of luxury and ease. Protected by his father from the realities of suffering and death, he assumed that his life journey would flow comfortably from a privileged childhood and young adulthood and then to political power and national leadership. Like many young people, he also assumed that he was invulnerable, until the day he encountered an old man, toothless and bent over, and recognized for the first time the realities of aging. The next day he encountered a person wracked with disease and discovered for the first time the realities of physical suffering and illness. On the third day he encountered a corpse and realized that death is the ultimate horizon for humankind, including himself. As the story goes, on the fourth day this young man encountered a monk carrying a begging bowl and realized that there was a spiritual pathway to experiencing peace in a world of constant change. In facing the realities of aging, sickness, and death, Siddhartha Gautama took the first steps on his journey to become the Buddha, the enlightened one. His commitment to spiritual transformation amid the realities of suffering and loss enabled him to transform his feelings of dislocation and uncertainty into transformational healing and service.

Jesus of Nazareth, like Gautama, also embraced the reality of suffering and transformed it by demonstrating concretely over and over again that life, not death and suffering, has the last word. Nevertheless, this healing word is given not by the avoidance of suffering and death but by embracing them with faith, hope, and love. Jesus's embrace of God's presence in the midst of human pain released energies that healed mind, body, spirit, and relationships.[1]

In his interpretation of the Psalms, Old Testament scholar Walter Brueggemann portrays a similar pathway from initial comfort to vulnerability and eventually to wholeness and healing. For some people, Brueggemann notes, life flows pleasantly and comfortably. In this state of orientation, the bills are paid, relationships are healthy and satisfying, vocation is meaningful, and health is taken for granted. But nothing lasts forever—in the midst of a good and predictable life, a phone call reports a parent's stroke, a medical test reveals cancer, a child is diagnosed with mental illness, a painful childhood memory surfaces, the stock market collapses and with it precious retirement funds, and the company downsizes, discharging the majority of its middle managers and assembly line workers. All of sudden we are thrown into a world of disorientation in which there are no certainties and few supports. Our perception of the dependability and goodness of life, as well as the meaning of our lives, is shattered as we simply try to make it through the challenges of the day and maintain enough hope to plan for a radically changed future. It is precisely in this disorientation that we may encounter the surprising grace of God: our prayers are finally answered, relief comes, or we discover strength and resources to deal creatively with what cannot be changed. Although our lives will never be the same as they were before the crisis, we can experience a new orientation that embraces life and death, health and illness, success and failure, and grace and sin.[2] This new orientation, the two of us believe, is the gift of God's intimate companionship through the love and support of others and a lively life of prayer, which provide new and creative possibilities for personal, relational, and community transformation when we otherwise would see only dead ends.

At the time we conceived this text, we began a family journey that would take us through our own path of orientation, disorientation, and new orientation. When our recently married twenty-seven-year-old son, Matt, was diagnosed with a rare type of cancer in October 2007, we discovered firsthand the reality that that you cannot go around the valley of pain and desolation; you must go through it if you are to experience healing and wholeness. While we will be in this valley until our son is pronounced fully cured after five years without further cancerous growth, this challenging journey has ultimately deepened our commitment to sensitively and creatively journey with vulnerable people facing life-threatening illnesses and their families. Through this time of disorientation and new orientation, we have experienced God's presence in friends' companionship, intimate moments in the chemotherapy ward, and visions of possibilities for life and love that called us from fear to hope.

Episcopal priest and spiritual director Alan Jones notes that spiritual direction deals with life's "unfixables."[3] Similarly, pastoral care also deals with those unfixable events of life, whether dramatic or chronic, that force both pastors and parishioners to face their limits, vulnerability, and mortality. Just as the pastor's calling to be a spiritual guide inspires his own commitment to spiritual growth through practices of prayer and meditation, the pastor's call to share in people's vulnerability and pain calls her to face squarely her own experiences of brokenness, pain, hopelessness, grief, and mortality. Sometimes, as in our family's experience last year, there is no avoiding them, but we believe that our commitment to embracing the disorienting dimensions of ministry with others throughout the years prepared us to face the challenges of our own family's journey as well as enriched our life and work on a daily basis.

In this chapter, we invite you to explore what it means to practice the presence of God in pastoral care with vulnerable people through examining and consecrating your greatest vulnerabilities and fears in light of God's presence. Our goal is not to describe in detail the many pastoral care challenges that ministers face within congregations, but to invite pastors to become healers in process who trust God's fidelity as they walk with their parishioners "through the darkest valley" (Ps. 23:4).

In this chapter, we will focus on developing one's personal and relational stature as an essential component of effective and empathetic pastoral care. Within this context we will consider the importance and dynamics of *radical acceptance* and *healing intentionality* in pastoral care relationships.

A Pastor of Sufficient Stature

Throughout this book, we have noted that practicing the presence of God in ministry is a way of life rather than just one more subject or skill a pastor needs to learn. By making a commitment to experiencing the dynamic and relational God more fully in his pastoral encounters, a minister soon discovers God's presence in what he may consider the least likely and most routine aspects of ministry. Holistic spiritual practices such as prayer, meditation, self-care, holy reading, study, and sabbath awaken our hearts to God's presence in the mundane as well as the dramatic moments of ministry. We discover that God's lively and transforming grace is both universal and intimate. The living God presents us with visions for each moment and for our lifetime. But, ultimately, practicing the presence of God is a matter of graceful responsiveness to God's constant and evolving call in our lives. Awakening to God's evolving visions for our lives and congregations enables us to consecrate each moment—that is, make each moment a holy and wholly alive gift to God and our world. In every ministerial encounter, a spirit-centered pastor is challenged to remember Samuel's prayer, "Speak, for your servant is listening" (1 Sam. 3:10). A commitment to listen prayerfully for God's voice in your own body-mind-spirit experience and in the lives of those with whom you minister opens you to new and unexpected possibilities that will change everything in your personal and professional life as a pastor.

Holistically practicing the presence of God in ministry enables us to prepare and to respond to various dramatic and ongoing pastoral care crises. A life devoted to prayerful attentiveness to God's lively presence in our bodies as well as our minds opens us to unexpected guidance in responding with care and sensitivity to unexpected deaths, traumatic situations of grief and loss, and life-threatening illnesses among our congregants. Such prayerful awareness also enables spiritual leaders to minister patiently and creatively with chronic issues of mind, body, emotion, and spirit. Each encounter can be a potential theophany, a moment when God appears to us within the guise of another's physical and emotional pain. As pastoral care professor Gordon Jackson notes, "God does not need to be bootlegged into a caring or counseling conversation. God is in the situation!"[4] Pastoral theologian Edward Wimberly counsels pastors to "trust God's presence in the counseling session."[5] God is here, embodied in your life and the one with whom you are ministering, giving you insights into ways you can respond in a healing way.

Take a few moments to review your pastoral care ministry and your vocation as God's healing partner in moments of challenge and pain. Listening to your life as a pastor, we ask you to consider: Where have you experienced God's presence in response to the pain of another? Where has your understanding of God been challenged and transformed as a result of a congregant's questions about the meaning of suffering or God's role in health and illness? Where have you experienced God's presence in people with whom you have ministered in times of transition and crisis?

Process-relational theologian Bernard Loomer, with whom Bruce studied, believed that size or stature was among the most essential spiritual and theological virtues. According to Loomer, spiritual and theological stature involves our ability to embrace as much of reality as possible, including contrast and contradiction, and joy and depression, without losing our personal center. Loomer defined a person's stature in terms of

*the range and depth of his [or her] love, his [or her] capacity
for relationships. I mean the volume of life you can take into
your being and still maintain your integrity and individual-
ity, the intensity and variety of outlook you can entertain in
the unity of your being without feeling defensive or insecure . . .
the strength of your spirit to encourage others to become fre-
er in the development of their diversity and uniqueness . . .
the magnanimity of concern to provide conditions to enable others
to increase in stature.*[6]

Stature is not just a matter of our ability to entertain a variety
of theological perspectives. It involves our openness to experiencing another person's emotional life by opening to their body
as well as their emotions as reflective of the dynamic interplay
of pain and healing.

A person of professional and spiritual stature can embrace
stories of pain and hopelessness, let go of the need to fix situations, accept others' anger and anguish, and even unbelief, while
maintaining an open heart and a nonanxious presence.[7] The
two of us believe that pastors become God's healing partners
when we follow the way of Jesus; we grow in wisdom and stature through integrating holistic spiritual practices and theological reflection with pastoral care skills in responding to the
realities of trauma, bereavement, chronic illness, mental health
issues, sickness, and death.

Spiritual stature involves the dynamic interplay of radical
acceptance and healing intentionality. On the one hand, *radical
acceptance* involves empathetically identifying with the experiences of others and claiming our own experiences as completely
as possible without judgment, fear, or revulsion, while remain-
ing grounded and aware of our authentic responses to these
experiences. On the other hand, *healing intentionality* enables
us to see our presence in every pastoral encounter as a crucible
for creative and healing transformation. The lively interplay of
radical acceptance and healing intentionality in pastoral care

joins the virtues of contemplation and action, listening and responding, letting go and moving forward, and fluidity and boundary keeping that are characteristic of God's holy adventure in our lives.

In pastoral care, radical acceptance is anything but passive. To listen completely to another and claim the fullness of your own experience in response requires tremendous effort and focus. As one pastor notes, "When I'm really in touch with a person's pain, all my senses are working. I can literally *feel* my congregant's joy or pain and physical comfort or discomfort with what they are sharing. After the appointment is over, I often need to take a walk or meditate to recharge my own spiritual energy." Healing intentionality arises from our awareness of the subtle movements of God's healing presence in the other's life situation rather than our own need to fix things or achieve a particular result.

In many ways, growing in spiritual and pastoral stature reflects Jesus's counsel to his followers to "be perfect, therefore, as your heavenly [Parent] is perfect" (Matt. 5:48). Here *perfection* means wholeness of spirit and not perfectionism. This sense of wholeness allows us to embrace reality as it is, including God's vision and energy of healing in each situation. Like Jesus, we must face and deal with our own personal temptations and wounds in order to be faithful to God's call to wholeness and fidelity in our personal and professional lives.

Growing in wisdom and stature is a theological as well as a spiritual issue that beckons us to experience God's overarching lure toward healing and wholeness in all things and, in particular, God's ever-present, lively healing possibilities in every situation of need and brokenness. For the two of us, the quest for stature in pastoral care reflects our vision of God's dynamic, creative, and responsive love. As the one "to whom all hearts are open and all desires known" (Book of Common Prayer), God experiences and embraces the totality of *our experience* as part of God's own vision of personal and corporate justice and wholeness. God responds in light of the needs of particular individuals in their unique situations, inspiring the quest for beauty and wholeness regardless of their particular physical, emotional, spiritual, or relational variables.

Because of God's constant and graceful lure toward creative transformation, we pastors can let go of our compulsions to fix difficult situations. We can trust that God will provide a way when there is no way, both for us and for those to whom we minister. As pastoral caregivers trusting this ever-present healing force, we are comforted and guided in such a way that we realize we are never alone, nor are the people who come to us in all their pain, anger, and uncertainty. God's acceptance, affirmation, and possibility encircle and embrace pastor and congregant alike. We can take heart in remembering the words of an anonymous Christian mystic, "God is the circle whose center is everywhere, and whose circumference is nowhere." God is working in our lives and also in the lives of those with whom we minister.

The Ministry of Radical Acceptance

The story is told of a woman who came to Gautama Buddha carrying her recently deceased child. Beside herself with grief, she begged the Buddha to restore her child to life. The Enlightened One responded with a task—"Go into the village and find a mustard seed, but this mustard seed must come from a household unaffected by death, whether that of a parent, grandparent, spouse, child, sibling, or favorite pet." Hours later the woman returned to the Buddha with the vow to enter the spiritual path, for she had not been able to find a household unaffected by death. She realized the universality of death and suffering. In this spirit, pastoral care professor Peggy Way notes that people choosing the ministry "frequently do not realize that they are choosing a lifetime of preoccupation with death in its many forms."[8] Yet, if we are to be God's healing partners following the way of Jesus, we must be willing to face all of life's tragedies with an open heart and accepting spirit.

Every long-term pastor has walked through the valley of mortality and illness with scores of parishioners. These experiences of limitation and sickness remind us of our own utter vulnerability and death's unspoken reality that shapes the living of our days. In this context, our primary task is to remember (re-member) what author Parker Palmer calls the "hidden wholeness" that undergirds our lives and the lives of those with whom we minister and also to deal with our own personal wounds and questions.[9]

Just think a moment of your own ministry. In the last month, how often have you prayed with a congregant and her family prior to surgery? How often has a congregant shared with you the news of a negative medical report, either his own, a friend's, or a relative's? How often have you sat with a grieving spouse or visited a congregant suffering from Alzheimer's disease or living with some other chronic, debilitating chronic or terminal illness? How often have you walked to your car, pondering, "Where is God in this situation?" How often have you experienced a sense of helplessness in your efforts to respond to trauma, bereavement, or mental illness? How often has a congregant asked in her own particular way one of the essential theological questions, Why am I suffering like this? Why is God doing this to me? What I have I done wrong to deserve this anguish?

Consider your response in such a situation. All too often we emotionally shut down when a question hits too close to home and we haven't done our emotional and spiritual processing. If you admit, as all of us have, that at times you have shut down, what is the spiritual and emotional work you are called to do related to that particular subject? On the other hand, take a few moments to ponder when you have been most effective as a pastoral caregiver and you have experienced and mediated hope and new life in the midst of personal distress and disorientation. How have you been able to empathetically build bridges of hope to others?

The quest to practice God's presence in pastoral care calls us to cultivate self-awareness in ministry's difficult situations. Healthy and compassionate pastoral care invites us to know ourselves, including those areas of personal pain and vulnerability that may shape the quality of our ministry with people experiencing certain mental, physical, emotional, or relational conditions. Acceptance of the fullness of our experience enables us to become, as Henri Nouwen asserted, wounded healers whose own commitment to embracing our own vulnerability and pain enables us to mediate God's healing touch to others.[10]

Tara Brach, clinical psychologist and Buddhist meditation teacher, describes the practice of radical acceptance as learning to experience the world "with an open heart" and "mindfulness and compassion" toward oneself and others. The liberating pathway of radical acceptance "begins with *accepting absolutely everything* about our lives, by embracing with wakefulness and care our moment-by-moment experience," including our thoughts, emotional responses, and feelings. According to Brach, self-acceptance "means feeling sorrow and pain without resisting. It means feeling desire or dislike for someone or something without judging ourselves for the feeling or being driven to act on it."[11] This is not moral relativism but God's grace in action, embodied in Gerald May's counsel to *pause, notice, open, yield and stretch,* and *respond*. In allowing God to be graceful toward us amid our own feelings of ambivalence, hopelessness, and doubt, we experience open-hearted grace toward others.

Having a listening, open heart that responds empathetically to suffering and loss is at the center of effective pastoral care. However, our fear most prevents us from dealing with the pain of others. Feelings of fear and impotence close off the heart quicker than anything else. But, as the Scriptures proclaim, our awareness of God's love enables us to face our fears. It is no coincidence that angelic visitations are most often accompanied by the words, "Do not be afraid." Facing and working through our fears is an important part of growing in stature and maturity as a pastor.

Fear often comes in many disguises. The senior pastor of a midsized, multigenerational congregation, Ed found himself dragging his feet or delegating hospital visits to the associate pastor whenever the hospitalized person was someone with a life-threatening illness. One day his associate asked him point blank, "Why don't you ever visit people with cancer? Do you have a problem with death?" As he reflected on his colleague's remark, he realized that he was still grieving his father's unexpected death from pancreatic cancer several years earlier. "I really hadn't given myself a chance to grieve when my father died," Ed admitted. "I was asked to conduct his funeral and a week after his death, there were two deaths from cancer in my congregation and I felt that I needed to be present at the deathbed and in comforting the family. I guess I just shut down emotionally. I was there in body but not in spirit. I guess I've been shut down ever since. I never realized that I may have short-circuited my own tears and grief." Following this realization, Ed chose to enter counseling not just to support his pastoral ministry but also to claim the whole range of emotions that he had been suppressing as a result of unhealed grief. When we suppress or deny one area of our emotional life, the whole range of our emotional life suffers.

After a few months, Ed noted, "Now I can feel joy again, and I'm beginning to minister with a whole heart. I feel comfortable with tears and laughter, even my own, when I am responding to families facing a loved one's impending or recent death. I am grateful that my associate was courageous enough to share his insights."

In a similar fashion, Samantha felt uncomfortable and generally avoided dealing directly with women and men who had experienced childhood sexual trauma. She had never taken the time to emotionally and spiritually work through the complex and painful dynamics of being the victim of pastoral misconduct as a teenager. "In facing my own pain with a trusted professional colleague, I experienced God's healing and, out of that healing, I discovered a special calling to minister with men and women who have experienced childhood sexual abuse."

The two of us believe that all pastors need to pursue a high level of intentionality in integrating our intellectual, spiritual, and emotional experiences in order to effectively share God's healing touch in our pastoral care ministries. Raised in a conservative, biblically centered, American Baptist household, Bruce—despite his progressive theological outlook—struggled for years with fully accepting gay, lesbian, bisexual, and transgendered people as individuals of equal worth and giftedness in the eyes of God. He also wrestled with his challenging relationship with his gay brother. Although Bruce first responded to his discomfort with homosexuality by studying Scripture and theological writings related to gay and lesbian issues, his intellectual journey needed to be complemented by an equally thorough spiritual adventure involving prayerful acceptance of his brother's sexuality and open-hearted acceptance of gay and lesbian people with whom he ministered and worked. In awakening to and accepting his own homophobia, Bruce experienced God's healing touch that enabled him to become an ally not only of LGBTQ people but also of the copastor serving a congregation open and affirming of LGBTQ people.[12] Bruce confesses that his experience of healing resulted, first, from accepting his discomfort with gay men and, most particularly, his brother, and then truly seeking the gift of an open and compassionate heart. Bruce's healing involved the journey inward and the journey outward, a commitment to prayer, meditation, and study, complemented by active involvement as a friend and colleague with gay and lesbian people.

Radical acceptance of the totality of our experience is one of the greatest antidotes to the compassion fatigue that is epidemic among ministers, counselors, physicians, and nurses. Compassion fatigue results from the emotional overload of dealing with too many emotionally charged situations at one time. According to psychologist Linda Schupp, caregivers who respond regularly to people who have experienced trauma or post-traumatic stress are at risk of compassion fatigue. Compassion fatigue occurs when people are "continually exposed to extreme circumstances whether directly or indirectly, in an attempt to treat or support traumatized people." Schupp maintains that since the effects of compassion fatigue are cumulative, caregivers, such as pastors, may be "unaware of this syndrome's ability to rob them of their energy, vitality, and resiliency." When we fail to accept the totality of our experience, including our feelings of pain, helplessness, and stress, we pastors run the risk of "sacrificing [our] own physical, mental, emotional, and spiritual well-being on the *altars of compassion*."[13] Healthy pastors know their limits in dealing with difficult pastoral care situations. Informed by their awareness of their own emotional stressors, they learn the virtues of self-care, retreat, collegial support, and referral when they begin to experience themselves as emotionally overloaded.

When our son was diagnosed with cancer at age twenty-seven, the two of us monitored our spiritual and emotional well-being and paced ourselves carefully. It took all the self-awareness and personal strength we could muster to face our pain as parents of a child with a life-threatening illness, and yet also care for ourselves, our congregants, our students, and other dependent family members. As we made ourselves spiritually and emotionally present to our son and his wife, we intentionally sought the support and comfort of friends, relatives, and colleagues, many of whom traveled hundreds of miles to be with us in our son's hospital room. Bruce found a quiet center amid the chaos of cancer treatments by committing himself to his regular spiritual practices of meditation, self-Reiki, and centering prayer, regardless of the stresses of the day. More of an extravert, Kate found moments of solace and peace on a regular basis through prayer shawl knitting, journaling, and checking in regularly with friends. We learned gently to say no to unnecessary professional commitments. Gracefully, the leadership of both Lancaster Theological Seminary and Disciples United Community Church understood our need to be present physically more often with our recently married son and his wife, Ingrid, even though we live two hours away from their home in Washington, DC. Both institutions made allowances for our absences and continue to support us with prayer as well as personal professional affirmations.

Now a year later, as we are writing these words, we still feel the traumatic impact of our son's cancer in our emotional lives as we await the results of his regular CT scans and blood work. We must remain mindful of the anxiety we still experience, though mostly unconscious, as we respond to serious illnesses among parishioners, friends, family members, and students. If we as pastoral caregivers were to deny the pain we experienced during our son's confrontation with cancer as well as the pain that still surfaces when we address people with life-threatening illnesses, our care for vulnerable people would become superficial and ultimately harmful to them and ourselves.

A few months after Matt's final chemotherapy treatment, we received a surprising affirmation during our congregation's mutual ministry review. One of the members commented, in speaking for the committee, that "Bruce and Kate showed us how to respond to serious illness with grace and care. You cared for your family, but also maintained the highest quality professional standards and care for this congregation."

The two of us recognize that we could not have creatively and lovingly integrated care for our son and his wife, support for Kate's ninety-one-year-old mother and Bruce's disabled brother, our own personal well-being, and our pastoral leadership without a large cloud of witnesses surrounding us in the form of nurturing friendships, caring institutions, and the prayers of people across the globe. Healthy interdependence, grounded in the recognition that we live in a dynamic web of relationships, palpably strengthens us at such times and reminds us that we are all in this together. We have come to realize that within the body of Christ, there is no ultimate distinction between giver and receiver, healthy and sick, pastor and layperson, caregiver and patient. When we face our own vulnerability and fear embraced by God's faithful companionship and the gifts of faithful friends and communities, we discover strength in our weakness and grace in our vulnerability. As we open prayerfully to God's inspiring and comforting companionship, our wounds become the media of God's healing touch to other vulnerable people.

The Ministry of Healing Intentionality

John's Gospel proclaims that Jesus's mission was grounded in the affirmation, "I came that they may have life, and have it abundantly" (John 10:10). God's quest for abundant life was manifest in Jesus's all-embracing ministry of healing, hospitality, and reconciliation. Jesus's vision of divine hospitality that guided his day-to-day encounters and overall ministry can guide us as well.

We who follow the way of Jesus are also challenged to holistically embody God's healing touch and quest for abundant life in every aspect of our compassionate leadership. Vulnerable people, whether facing health crises, loss and bereavement, trauma, or emotional upheaval, come to pastors in search of healing and wholeness. They recognize their own brokenness and seek, through regularly scheduled and carefully boundaried pastoral care with their pastor, the abundance of healing and wholeness that comes through God's intimate healing and guiding presence.

We believe that pastors, as representatives and mediators of God's abundant life, must seek to be open to God's healing intentionality in every pastoral care situation. Recognizing that each moment arises from a multitude of interdependent factors—including environment, DNA, physical and emotional condition, relationships, previous decisions, spiritual practices and the prayers of others—our embodiment of the healing presence of God can be and often is the tipping point towards experiencing God's dynamic healing presence. Working within all these factors, God seeks to guide, comfort, inspire, challenge, and energize those with whom we minister. This vision of the pastor's role in the healing process assumes that God's vision and aim toward healing and wholeness is always concrete, personal, and intimately related to each dynamic and unique moment of experience and every unique encounter. In the ecology of God's aim at healing, wholeness, and abundant life, our calling is to be open to God's vision both for us and for those with whom we pastor, for they are often synchronously interrelated. Accordingly, we need to listen carefully to the Spirit's "sighs too deep for words" in every pastoral care situation (Rom. 8:26). Within the commitment to radical acceptance of our experience in its entirety is also the openness to experience and follow God's vision of health and wholeness that resides in each moment.

Jesus's healing ministry serves as a model for the healing intentionality necessary for the pastoral care of others.[14] First, Jesus sought abundant life for everyone he encountered. Jesus realized that God's aim at abundant life varied from situation to situation and person to person. His prescriptions for healing varied widely. Jesus bids Zaccheus to come down from a tree and share a meal. For this corrupt and despised tax collector, the path to abundant life involved making amends with those he cheated in the past and becoming a channel of divine generosity (Luke 19). The healing of Mary of Bethany involved Jesus's willingness to let her cross gender and economic boundaries by anointing his feet (John 12:1–8). Jesus challenged a man who had spent a lifetime waiting for a healing to stand up and walk (John 5:1–9). In encountering a man who was blind from birth, Jesus performed a theological healing, releasing the man and his parents from the burden of blame and self-reproach (John 9:1–8). Open to God's desire for abundant life in every situation, Jesus concretely joined acceptance of people in need with a spirit-filled vision that would encourage them to awaken God's healing touch in their lives.

Jesus's approach to healing is a model for our own healing intentionality. Jesus employed a variety of healing practices appropriate to each particular person, time, and place. Led by his deep understanding of God's creative wisdom, Jesus responded to people's healing needs through touch, energy, words, faith, challenge, question, forgiveness, hospitality, mud and saliva, and distant prayer, and we can use many of these modalities today. In sync with God's vision for each encounter, Jesus mediated God's healing touch in noncoercive and life-transforming ways. Those who follow the way of Jesus are not limited to *one* approach to human wholeness, but can employ *any* appropriate healing methodology in response to human need. But in order to know what approach will most creatively mediate God's aim at healing and abundance, we must carefully and intuitively listen for God's presence amid the dynamic interplay of our lives and the lives of those to whom we minister.

Discerning God's vision for healing and wholeness in any situation is always challenging because God's vision is always embedded in the particularity of each situation and is revealed not *beyond* our experience but *within* the totality of our encounters and our response to them. God comes to us within the world of our experience in all its complexity. This means that God's wisdom rarely comes to us in an absolutely clear moment of discernment. While we can never entirely get our self-interest out of the way, we can pray constantly for divine wisdom and guidance and that in every situation God's desire for healing and abundant life will be realized. Although many of us, especially people with extroverted personalities, receive our greatest insights in talking with others, awareness of God's vision in each pastoral situation, including lively conversations, also requires a life committed to *pausing, noticing, opening, yielding and stretching,* and then *responding* to God's presence. While we trust God's guidance, we must also remember that the treasures we receive and our experiences of divine guidance are always delivered in earthen vessels. Knowing that we always see in a mirror dimly, our first task is to humbly create an open space where both we and our pastoral companions can awaken to the subtle movements of God in our lives in the present moment.

Healing intentionality can take many forms. It may be reflected in pausing to ask simple but life-changing questions, such as the question Jesus asked of a man who had sat nearly four decades a the pool in Jerusalem waiting for a miracle: "Do you want to be made well?" (John 5:6). It may also be reflected in expressing realistic and affirming statements such as "God is present in your life and God will give you the guidance and strength you need," or "You are God's beloved daughter." God's healing presence can also be mediated through the simple act of listening without comment or judgment to one who has been censored, and self-censored, throughout his life, or through welcoming someone into your life who feels unworthy of God's love. It may also come through the interplay of confession and forgiveness in which the pastor, speaking God's word of grace and transformation, says, "God forgives you. I forgive you. Now, forgive yourself and commit yourself to a life of faithfulness, courage, and integrity."

Healing intentionality always involves spacious acceptance, but radical acceptance may also involve challenging people to become a new creation. Theologian and pastor Rebecca Parker tells the story of her pastoral encounter with a woman named Lucia who had been victimized by an abusive husband for more than two decades. Lucia had remained in a violent marriage because of the counsel her priest had given her. According to Lucia, her priest had said "I should rejoice in my sufferings because they bring me closer to Jesus. . . . If you love Jesus, accept the beatings and bear them gladly, as Jesus bore the cross." Now that her children were being threatened, Lucia began to question the priest's counsel.

Parker's response to Lucia joined the prophetic vision of an alternative reality with the realistic acceptance of the woman's current life situation. Parker did not judge Lucia but listened deeply for God's voice of liberation and empowerment. Indeed, Parker's counsel to Lucia emerged from deep spiritual listening as well as healthy theological reflection. Parker remembers that "in the stillness of the moment, I could see in Lucia's eyes that she knew the answers to her question, just as I did." After a reflective pause, Parker provided a heartfelt theological alternative to the life-destroying theology Lucia had received many years earlier: "God doesn't want you to accept being beaten by your husband. God wants you to have your life, not give it up. God wants to protect your life and your children's lives."[15]

Radical acceptance joined with healing intentionality requires patience with those with whom we minister, with ourselves, and with God, since many problems are chronic or cannot be fixed and will be resolved only after long and difficult struggles. Pastoral caregivers are called to take heart in Jesus's parable of the mustard seed. Great things often begin quietly and slowly, and the healing process is often imperceptible even for those to whom it is occurring. Our companionship with congregants over weeks and months may be the tipping point in which seemingly glacial change gives birth to life-transforming quantum leaps.

Every healing companion is challenged to frame her or his ministry using the model of the following healing encounter, described in Mark's Gospel:

> Some people brought a blind man to him and begged him to touch him. He took the blind man by the hand and led him out of the village; and when he had put saliva on his eyes and laid hands on him, he asked him, "Can you see anything?" And the man looked up and said, "I can see people, but they look like trees, walking." Then Jesus laid his hands on his eyes again; and he looked intently and his sight was restored, and he saw everything clearly (Mark 8:22–25).

When Jesus's first attempt to cure the man of blindness did not fully succeed, Jesus did not blame the man for his lack of faith; nor did Jesus tell him that his deferred healing was God's will or intended to strengthen his faith. Jesus did not make up excuses for his failure to complete the healing or give up on the sight-impaired man. He continued to minister to the man until the man experienced the cure that he and Jesus sought. We cannot predict or control the timetable of healing. Rather, we must trust that God is working in us and others, seeking the greatest wholeness and beauty of experience that is possible in each person's life.

Awakening to God's healing intentionality calls us to distinguish between curing and healing. According to philosophers and socioogists of medicine, *curing* relates to the elimination of symptoms, for example, recovering from a summer cold, the lifting of depression, the mending of a broken bone, or being cancer-free after five years. *Healing* relates to a sense of peace and divine presence that we can experience even when a physical or emotional cure is elusive. When the apostle Paul proclaims that nothing can separate us from the love of God (Rom. 8:39), he frames his affirmation in terms of those realities that are ultimately out of our control—situations such as death, political persecution, famine. The experience of peace emerges in our personal and community lives when we discover God's faithful presence in those realities that we cannot change as well as God's inspiration to transform what is in our power.

A number of years ago an active Episcopalian lay woman sought Bruce out for spiritual direction. Her compelling question involved the focus of her intercessory prayers. "My dear friend has cancer. For a while, I prayed a cure, but now it seems that this prayer has not been answered. She is in great pain, and death would be a relief. I feel guilty now that I am praying for a peaceful death rather than a cure." After a few hours of conversation, she realized that she was not, in fact, praying for her friend's death, but that her new prayer focus involved the quest for spiritual healing for herself and a gentle and painless death for her friend. She discovered that when there cannot be a cure, there can always be a healing, that is, an intimate and life-transforming sense of God's great faithfulness and love, mediated through loving communities that provide comfort in every season of living and dying.

Spiritually centered pastoral care has one goal, reflected in many ways—the experience of God's healing presence and the peace, beauty, and abundant life that flow from companionship with the one whose love embraces life, death, and beyond. We practice the presence of God in pastoral care by attentiveness and awakening to the whole of life, including God's loving vision incarnate in every moment of sorrow or joy.

Contemplation and Compassion

Matthew 14 describes the interplay of contemplation and compassion in Jesus's ministry of healing and care. After Jesus hears of the murder of John the Baptist, the scripture notes that "he withdrew from there in a boat to a deserted place by himself" (Matt. 14:13). While Matthew does not provide us with details about Jesus's inner life, the perceptive reader can intuit that Jesus was grief stricken at the death of his lifelong spiritual companion and relative. John was more than a fellow religious teacher for Jesus. He was the spiritual leader who baptized Jesus, the companion with whom he played and contemplated the truths of faith as the two boys grew from childhood into adulthood. Perhaps Jesus and John studied together as they learned the deeper truths of their faith tradition. They may have theologically sparred over how to proclaim the message of the coming realm of God. We can even imagine John the Baptist being the first person with whom Jesus shared his temptations in the wilderness and the growing certainty that he was called to be God's messenger to the world. Jesus and John may have been partners in mutual spiritual direction. With the death of John the Baptist, Jesus may have felt as if he had lost his closest spiritual peer. The loss must have been great for the Healer of Nazareth.

While the Gospel does not reveal the time frame of Jesus's retreat, it suggests that Jesus's time apart was sufficient for him to experience his own spiritual healing and renewal. Refreshed by his retreat experience, Jesus greets the crowds with compassion rather than fatigue. He responds with energy and power to their physical and spiritual needs, and even anticipates their need for a good meal.

Many readers fail to grasp the profundity of what Jesus does immediately after teaching and feeding of the multitude. Wedged between two activist miracle stories are these words of counsel to every energetic and committed pastor: "Immediately [after feeding the multitude] he made the disciples get into the boat and go on ahead to the other side, while he dismissed the crowds. And after he had dismissed the crowds, he went up the mountain by himself to pray. When evening came, he was there alone" (Matt. 14:22–24). Could it be that Jesus recognized his own ability to mediate God's healing touch and proclaim the good news of God's coming realm depended on his putting his own spiritual well-being at the forefront, at least for a while?

The two of us believe that there are no throwaway lines in the Gospels. The author of Matthew's Gospel must have realized the spiritual and emotional demands the early Christians would face as the way of Jesus spread across an often antagonistic culture. We believe that the author of Matthew may well have recorded Jesus's two contemplative retreats as a model for healthy, energetic, and faithful spiritual leadership in challenging times.

Today's pastoral caregivers are challenged to embody Jesus's commitment to times of retreat and contemplative prayer, especially as they experience the stress of compassionately responding to people who are living with serious or chronic illness, bereavement, trauma, abuse, or vocational uncertainty.

Julie, a United Methodist pastor in the Washington, DC, suburbs, confesses that after years of struggle with issues of prayer and self-care, she finally understood the importance of spiritual retreat for pastoral care. "When I first entered the ministry, I felt guilty when I took time for study, retreat, and self-care. I rationalized my nonstop caregiving by saying to myself, 'Jesus would keep on going. Jesus would always be available to anyone who sought his attention.' But after months of seven-day work weeks, I knew that something had to change. I would either burn out or get sick if I didn't take a spiritual retreat and time simply to rest." Julie forced herself to go on a two-day silent retreat where she immersed herself in the Gospels. Looking for guidance, she discovered anew the wisdom of Matthew 14 and its companion passage, Mark 6:30–44. Julie confesses, "When I was meditating on these words, I realized that I was trying to 'outdo' Jesus in pastoral care. I realized that Jesus did take time off from ministry, and so could I! Jesus wasn't always on duty and at everyone's beck and call. Jesus knew when he needed to let go of his ministerial duties and simply rest in God's love." This insight transformed Julie's pastoral care ministry. Now she regularly goes on spiritual retreats and takes time to pray before and after every pastoral encounter. She regularly monitors and cares for her health of mind, body, spirit, and relationship.

Julie embodies what we have described as mindfulness in ministry. She pauses to notice the condition of her emotional, physical, relational, and spiritual life on a regular basis. When she notices her emotional life shutting down and her ability to listen to others compromised, she retreats, even if just for a few minutes, to revitalize and recover her spiritual center. "Sometimes, when I know that I am reaching my limit, I call ahead to tell my secretary or someone I may be meeting for a pastoral care appointment that I will be few minutes late. Then, I may just stop at the local coffeehouse to sip a latte and read a few pages of a devotional book I carry with me in the car. Or I may pull over at a local park, put on the walking shoes that I carry in backpack, and take a quick walk around the track. If I'm stressed out or emotionally fatigued, I know that I will do more harm than good for someone in need of healing."

It may seem strange to some pastors to realize that Julie and many other pastors intentionally prepare themselves for the inevitable moments of compassion fatigue and stress. They carry their spiritual and self-care equipment with them in anticipation that they may need to take a spiritual or emotional time-out in order to respond with compassion to the pastoral care needs of others. Like Jesus the healer, their compassionate pastoral care emerges from a life of engagement and withdrawal that will sustain them even in the most challenging pastoral situations.

Practicing the Presence of God in Pastoral Care

As we have stated above, practicing the presence of God in pastoral care means making a commitment to joining radical acceptance with healing intentionality in every pastoral encounter. By practicing disciplined openness to the wholeness of their experience, we believe that pastors can become healthy mediators of God's healing touch to people in need.

Awakening to Your Life Experience

Many of us are so busy in our ministry that we fail to attend to our own moment-by-moment experience. Yet, it is in these moments that God can truly work with us and through us. This exercise will help you develop awareness of your feelings and responses in the course of your ministerial encounters.

Throughout the day, pause a moment and open to the experience of the present moment. Without any self-judgment, take a moment to stop and feel your body. Kate often suggests the following to her spiritual directees at the beginning of a session: Breathe deeply and gently into your belly, and as you breathe, drop your body awareness downward, all the way to your toes. Wiggle your toes and feel the floor beneath your feet. Take time to notice your large muscle groups, releasing any tension or soreness.

Take time to breathe deeply, inhaling the goodness of life and exhaling the stresses in your life. Are you in touch with the present moment? If not, continue to ground yourself by gently attending to your breath, using your awareness of inhaling and exhaling as a way of opening and yielding to God. Then, when you feel ready, notice your emotional state. Have your most recent pastoral care appointments raised any feelings of past grief, suffering, loss, or trauma? What fears and anxieties might be stirring within you?

You may choose to take a few more moments for prayer and contemplation, yielding any pain, uneasiness, or fear to the companionship of God's wisdom. Under certain circumstances, the best response to unexpected or recently surfaced emotional pain may involve canceling pastoral care or congregational business appointments in order to provide sufficient time to regain your sense of pastoral equanimity and openheartedness through whatever self-care practices work best for you. The holiness of our pastoral vocation calls us to be at our best when we are addressing congregants' serious theological, spiritual, relational, or emotional issues. If we do not feel we can be spiritually and emotionally attentive, it is best that we reschedule to another time.

Often pastoral encounters raise painful memories that we have repressed, denied, or forgotten. If these memories point to deep and unhealed experiences of trauma, abuse, or grief, the two of us advise you to seek professional care with a pastoral counselor or psychotherapist sensitive to issues of compassion fatigue and secondary trauma experienced by pastors and other professional caregivers.

Embracing Suffering in the Spirit of Christ

Tara Brach recommends the Tibetan Buddhist practice *tonglen*, "taking in and sending out," as a pathway to radical acceptance. According to Brach, "linked to the flow of breath, this practice trains you to open directly to suffering—your own and all beings—and offer relief and care."[16] Buddhist meditation begins with breathing in suffering and breathing out wholeness. In contrast, a Christian approach to tonglen has three steps— awakening to God's healing and protecting presence, opening to the suffering of the world, and releasing that suffering through an exhalation of healing breath.

In this exercise, take a few moments to breathe deeply, gently relaxing into God's loving presence. Experience the intimacy of God, the life-sustaining reality in whom you live and move and have your being. If you wish to personify God's presence, you might visualize yourself surrounded by God's healing light, a parent's or companion's loving arms, or embraced by Jesus the healer.

As you experience God's loving presence, bring to awareness a recent experience of pain in your own life. As you breathe in this moment of pain, let yourself feel its intensity and take an honest measure of its impact on your life. Hold onto this awareness of the pain a moment without judgment or denial. Then, with a gentle exhalation, release the pain to God. Trust God's ability to bring forth beauty and sensitivity, truth and compassion in God's good time, borne of the pain you experience.

As a second movement of the Spirit, either immediately following the above exercise or another contemplative practice through which you have grounded yourself, take a moment to visualize another's pain that you have recently witnessed. This can be the pain of family member, friend, or congregant. Resting in God's presence, empathetically breathe into that experience of pain and hold onto it for a moment, feeling their hurt and loss. Then, gently exhale, releasing and yielding the pain of another into God's healing presence, trusting that God will bring comfort and wholeness to those who suffer.

Finally, as a third movement of the Spirit, if you can maintain your contemplative focus, visualize the whole world in God's loving care. Visualize the suffering the world, either in the particular, such as the face of an Iraqi child, a parent in Darfur, or a member of the armed forces suffering from PTSD following her or his combat duty abroad. Breathe into the pain of these individuals. Whom do you visualize as you open yourself to experiencing solidarity with their suffering? Breathe out the pain you have empathetically experienced, yielding into the loving care of God, seeking to trust that God is with you in life and death, joy and suffering.

Praying Your Visits

Practicing healing intentionality involves our response to God's grace by "praying without ceasing" (1 Thess. 5:17). We can deepen our sense of God guiding our pastoral encounters if we enter each pastoral care appointment, whether scheduled or unscheduled, with a brief prayer, such as "Guide my thoughts, words, and actions in this moment," or "Spirit of the Living God, fall afresh on me." In pausing a moment for prayerful centering and holy breathing, we tap into a divine wisdom greater than our own and sufficient for every pastoral challenge.

Bruce often advises the pastors with whom he works to park their car at the far end of the hospital parking lot or a block away from a vulnerable congregant's home as a way of intentionally taking time for prayer and spiritual centering during their short walk. Kate advises hearty breath prayer, experienced in climbing the stairs rather than taking the elevator. The very act of prayerful walking or stair climbing invites us to experience God's resources in the present moment while helping us let go of any residual concerns from our previous appointments. Moments of prayerful preparation enable us to respond with greater centeredness and equanimity to anxious, grieving, and emotionally distraught congregants. In prayerful walking, we gain stature that will help us open to others' feelings while honoring our own experience in the midst of God's dynamic and ever-present love.

In the next two chapters, which focus on experiencing God's presence in administration, leadership, management, and prophetic hospitality, we continue to explore how pastors can remain spiritually centered, here looking at their public role as congregational and community leaders. In these public roles as well, we believe pastors can be more creative, effective, and transformative in their ministerial leadership when they cultivate experiences of God's presence through practices of prayer and meditation.

Contemplative Leadership and Administration

DISCOVERING GOD IN THE DETAILS

When he reflects on his role as the primary functional administrator of a two-hundred-member suburban congregation, Steve, now in his fifth year of ministry, confesses, "I never imagined that my call to ministry would involve running a small, struggling organization. The minute I enter the church office, I'm confronted with the most recent building maintenance crisis or a snafu in the setup of the upcoming church bazaar. Sadly, most days I have to address these details before I move on to the 'real' tasks that inspired me to enter ministry." Susan, for ten years the pastor of a midsized country parish in western Maryland, experiences the same dissonance between her sense of call and her daily duties as a building manager. "I don't have a regular secretary. So, when I come to church and discover that the basement is flooded after a rainstorm and there are only a few hours to spare before the senior citizens group, I pick up the phone and call the chair of trustees, and then start mopping the floor. If the building isn't ready, then we can't have a group and as the primary on-site person, I have to take charge or the place will be a mess."

Take a moment to reflect on your average pastoral day. How much time do you spend problem solving with issues relating to personnel, finances, or property? How often do you find yourself drawn into program and volunteer conflicts? How do these tasks shape the quality of your ministry and spiritual life?

On an average day, a pastor can find himself moving from proofreading the church newsletter, arranging for backup during the secretary's vacation, tracking down the chair of trustees about a long-neglected property issue, comparing church liability and property insurance policies, and checking to see if the bathrooms are clean, alongside responding to a family in crisis, preparing the worship service, reflecting on the scriptures for Sunday and writing his sermon, and discussing with the choir director a complaint about changes in the worship service.

Every pastor knows that God is in the details; but pastors have recognized the devil is also in the details. Whether or not we see administration as part of our calling as pastors, faithful and effective ministers recognize that administrative work has to be done, and our call is to bring spirit to the everyday and long-term tasks of administration. If we neglect the spiritual dimensions of administration, whether this involves dealing with church finances, property, strategic planning, or personnel and organizational management, we will eventually jeopardize our ability to be effective spiritual leaders of our congregations. Recognizing that ministry is a holistic and interdependent enterprise calls us to move with prayerful agility through what may appear at first glance to be dissonant tasks. Practicing the presence of God in ministry inspires us to discern our calling, in the spirit of Brother Lawrence, amid the "pots and pans" of financial statements, calls to the electrician, and volunteer and personnel management and program coordination. The challenge, as a newly ordained pastor of a small-town Presbyterian congregation notes, is to "find God right where I am and let go of my personal priorities in order to discover what God has in mind at the congregational board meeting or in workings of the church office."

For spirit-centered pastors, the quest for excellence in administration is not optional. While no one definition of administration exists, the two of us see administration as involving a pastor's overall role in shaping and guiding a congregation's mission through encouraging faithful excellence in congregational leadership, personnel, program, and physical infrastructure. Fidelity to the tasks of preparation, planning, and implementing enables pastors to gain their congregations' trust and provide for responding to their congregants' deepest spiritual and relational needs.[1]

In this chapter we will assume that administrative tasks are essentially spiritual in nature. Although there are many administrative roles, we will focus primarily on personnel and programmatic management and spiritual leadership as essential administrative tasks of ministry. These tasks require imaginative discernment in which our role is to help others see the forest amid the trees. In other words, the two of us will focus on ways pastors can work with congregants to see the details of church administration, both theirs and ours, within God's vision for the congregation and the wider community. Spiritually centered pastors are visionary leaders who seek to embody God's presence in (1) guiding a congregation toward its vision of God's calling and (2) actualizing the congregation's vision by promoting faithful excellence in the everyday, detail-oriented tasks of congregational life. Practicing the presence of God in administration involves spiritually grounded, creative strategic visioning and priority setting and program planning in light of our experience of God's vision of the congregation. In so doing, spiritually centered pastors nurture a sense of spiritual awareness and discernment among their congregants by embodying faithful and effective administration at every level of the congregation's life. Such pastors represent the spirit of appreciative reflection and affirmative administration.

Visionary Administration

Visionary administration? Now, that sounds like an oxymoron, doesn't it? All too often administration is identified with preserving the status quo, rearranging the deck chairs on the *Titanic*, or resisting the innovations necessary to move from maintenance to excellence. While the two of us believe that administration can atomize the best of us by its complexity and detail, we also believe that administration, like every other pastoral practice, can be profoundly spiritual and creative. We take our guidance from Proverbs 29:18 (KJV), "Where there is no vision, the people perish." From our perspective, administration, embracing both leadership and management, is the holistic practice of joining possibility with actuality, dreams with concrete situations, and visions with practical applications. We see administration as an active process involving creativity, imagination, and alignment with divine possibilities for the present moment and God's open future.

Healthy, vital, and transformative administration is grounded in the marriage of ongoing solid theological reflection and committed spiritual practice. Spiritually centered pastors are guided by a theological and pastoral vision that is embodied in every aspect of congregational management, leadership, and strategic planning. While there are many possible theological frameworks within which to conceive of administration, the two of us believe that practicing the presence of God in administration is best facilitated by ministering out of the theological affirmations that have guided this text:

1. God is present in all people, places, and things.
2. God's presence in the world is lively and always luring us toward a positive future.

3. God encourages creativity and imagination in people and institutions.

4. We live in a dynamically interdependent world in which everyone's life makes a difference.

The first affirmation reflects the traditional Christian belief that God is present everywhere and in all things. All places, people, and things reflect the creative wisdom of God. There are no God-forsaken places, tasks, or people. Accordingly, God can be served in any administrative task, whether it involves preparing and delivering a report for the church council or leadership team; mopping a floor in the wake of a heavy rainstorm; insuring that the congregation's gathering place is safe, attractive, and sanitary; or recruiting youth for a confirmation class. God is in the details of every pastoral task, including administration, because God is present and can be *experienced* as present in all things.

The second affirmation describes the nature of God's presence in the world and in our administrative tasks and individual and corporate futures. "God is still speaking," the slogan of the United Church of Christ, recognizes that God is constantly bringing forth new possibilities in our world. Believing in the God of infinite possibility invites us to make a space within our administrative tasks to nurture our imagination and contemplate God's new creation working in our congregations and pastoral ministry. Opening to God's possibilities calls us not only to look for manna in the desert and an abundant feast from a mere five loaves and two fish but also to believe we can create such abundance in times of great scarcity. While imaginative, spirit-filled administration is keenly aware of the very real financial and personnel limitations of congregations, imaginative administration also asserts that a congregation's limitations are the womb from which new possibilities emerge.

The third affirmation invites us to see spiritual life and administration as a part of God's ongoing creative process. Creation continues, whether in the birthing of solar systems or the emergence of new ways of doing old things. While ministerial creativity does not always insure growth in church membership or finances, openness to and faith in God's constant creativity call us to actively claim the core Christian truth that beyond every death is the promise of resurrection. The only dead ends in congregational life are those resulting from our lack of prayerful imagination.

The fourth affirmation proclaims the dynamic interdependence of life. Spiritual administration affirms the interdependent reality of the body of Christ and all its relationships. Spiritual administration promotes the development of healthy, creative, and life-transforming interpersonal relationships in which the pastor, holding appropriate pastoral boundaries, is both giver and receiver. In the intricate interdependence of life, we as pastors must affirm our need for mutually creative team relationships in ministry, which recognize and honor the gifts of laypeople of all ages, from infants to senior adults.

Leading with Vision and Care

The pastor of a struggling Lutheran congregation, Stephen wonders why so many of his ideas for congregational change seem to flounder as soon as the church board meeting concludes. "I have great ideas about where this church should be going. We need to launch a communitywide outreach program that includes evangelism and service to the area. This is the gospel mandate. Why doesn't my congregation get it?" Paula notes the same resistance to new and lively ideas among the lay leaders in the United Methodist congregation she serves. "If we're going to be a growing church, it is clear that we need to remodel the nursery, update the bathrooms, and make the building fully accessible. These changes need to be done now. We are at a tipping point! Why don't the trustees move ahead and do what's needed to grow this church? What's wrong with these people?"

The two of us believe that leadership involves the interplay of vision, persuasion, and concrete application. It also involves facing resistance creatively. Both Stephen and Paula are visionaries who have ideas that will transform their congregations, and while we don't know the whole story, the two of us believe that their visions are most likely stalled because they have not done the hard work of prayerful relationship building. They have forgotten that personal and congregational transformation is a concrete and relational process, which is birthed one personal relationship at a time. You can't be a visionary leader without the creative partnership of your congregation. You must not only plant the seed of possibility but also first cultivate and fertilize the soil through developing creative and trusting pastoral relationships. The body of Christ is not the pastor or the trustees or church board alone; it is the whole people of God prayerfully open and attentive to God's emerging vision for its particular time and place and its particular gifts and people. While the practice of spiritual discernment has its origins in the divine imagination, it finds its incarnation in the dynamic interrelatedness of everyday life in all its complexity and challenge. Dedicated pastoral leadership listens to God's presence in the "worst of these," those people with whom we disagree, and in the "least of these," those people whose pain and suffering also reveal the presence of God. Imaginative and prayerful pastors, seeking administrative change and growth, hear God's voice in resistance and in cooperation, and invite those who resist their vision to become partners in sharing in synergetic visions that embrace both novelty and tradition. This process, which we describe as appreciative and affirmative reflection, enables pastors to see the potential for growth in every congregational situation, including those involving resistance and conflict.

Clearly, we believe that pastoral administrative leadership is a spiritual practice involving both vision and care. Pastoral authority comes from many sources, including the experience of

call to ministry, the appropriate theological education, ministerial authorization or ordination, and the denominational and
congregational call process. But, this is only part of the story.
Ultimately, pastoral authority is grounded in the pastor's spiritual vitality and lively and concrete vision of the body of Christ,
lived out in holy relationships with the congregation. Visionary
administrative leadership is a holistic process in which a pastor's ability to lovingly know and understand her or his congregants is pivotal in discerning God's vision for the congregation's
future.

To the surprise of some take-charge leaders, Christian leadership begins with a pastor's "appreciative" stepping back to
undertake Gerald May's practice of *pausing, opening, noticing,
stretching and yielding,* and then *responding* to God's presence
in the congregation with a lively, contextual, and embodied
hope in the vision collectively given it. When we pastors pause,
open, and notice, we may experience divine revelation within
our congregation as being more like improvisational jazz, with
each instrument taking its turn to lead while others share their
voices in the background, than like the tune of a solo instrument. We may then be able to hear God's voice in those who
affirm the goodness of the way things always have been as well
as those who raise caution flags, calling us to consider the cost
of discipleship embedded in highly innovative programs.

We pastors are called to be the spiritual leaders and theologians of our congregations. Whether we like it or not, in
many cases, we are also the functional chief executive officers
of small but complex organizations of volunteers. Every young
pastor remembers the first time that he or she was asked at
board meeting, "Pastor, what do you think we should do about
the problem in the nursery?" Or, in a contentious discussion,
the pastor may be expected to have answers to questions such
as, "Will people from other faiths be saved or do they go to
hell?" or "How should we allocate the church's endowment?"
Our answers will never be right for everyone. Learning to wield

this power prayerfully and wisely takes practice. Whatever answer we give, our answer is never just private or personal, it shapes the whole community. More experienced pastors, after several years in the same congregation, discover much to their surprise that their weekly sermons really do make a difference, when they hear congregants sharing their theology in ways that mirror what they have heard hundreds of times from the pulpit.

Pastors are the spiritual leaders of congregations, and this fact cannot—and should not—be avoided. But the question the two of us pose to you in this text is, Will your administrative leadership deepen the spirituality of your congregation and your own spirituality, or will it be a source of conflict, fatigue, and frustration both for yourself and for the congregation? We believe that the form and style of your leadership and administration as a pastor cannot be separated from your theological beliefs and spiritual practices. Based on the theology and spirituality of administration we articulated in the previous section on visionary administration, the two of us see visionary leadership as a creative, appreciative, affirmative, and compassionate process that invites people to share actively in God's dream of healing, transformation, and growth in a congregation. Visionary leaders may show the pathway to God's future, but if our leadership is to be truly empowering to others, we must invite congregants to experience God's vision as they carry out their own varied and particular roles in the congregation's and community's life.

Therefore, we assert that visionary leadership is, first of all, *creative, appreciative, affirmative, and imaginative.* As leaders, we are called to be partners in bringing about the new creation God envisions for us and our congregations. We must listen simultaneously and deeply to God's presence in the church, the world, and our congregants. This discipline, which we call visionary and appreciative listening, awakens us to God's voice in the many voices of those around us. If God is indeed omnipresent, then all people reveal, to a greater or lesser degree, God's wisdom and insight. Creativity and vision, whether on the cosmic or congregational scales, are never isolated or individualistic but appreciatively take into account the concrete gifts, possibilities, and limitations of our environmental and social context. According to the first Genesis account of creation (Gen. 1:1–2:4a), even God must work with and also respond to the unique characteristics of the formless void. In that same spirit, visionary pastoral leadership is never *ex nihilo*—that is, creativity without context—but is always creation in relationship and partnership.

Visionary leadership is grounded in appreciating the concrete gifts and possibilities—as well as the limitations—of the congregation and pastor. Grounded in the affirmation of God's lively presence in all things, we believe that every congregation possesses a unique set of gifts *and* challenges. While some pastors and congregations turn their backs on their spiritual vocations, even in their turning away, we believe that God continues to call them toward faithful ministry in their time and place. In the spirit of appreciative inquiry, Mark Lau Branson notes "all organizations are heliotropic, rising toward health and joy."[2] Often, however, congregants and their spiritual leaders see only scarcity and disease and miss the fragile seeds of resurrection in their congregations. Imaginative leadership sees alternative possibilities to the scarcity thinking that often dominates congregational thinking. While visionary leadership does not insure congregational numerical growth or even, in the case of some declining congregations, long-term survival, it always looks for signs of fidelity, beauty, and commitment in challenging situations. This is not denial of a congregation's current financial or membership situation but attention to the deeper movements of God's new creation that reside in every situation.

Philosopher Alfred North Whitehead says that God is always providing contextual possibilities that are "the best for that [particular congregational] impasse."[3] While the "best for that impasse" may not be ideal and may even involve something as radical as eventually closing a congregation's doors, the visionary pastor claims God's resurrection power and life even in the face of institutional death and decline. Visionary leadership seeks the "best for that impasse" with the awareness that good-enough ministry like good-enough parenting can nurture and support the overall wholeness of congregations and children alike. Faithful ministry does not need to be successful by the world's standards; faithful leadership enables congregations, like individuals, to experience wholeness and grace in every season of their lifespan.

One practice that has shaped the sense of possibility in the two of us is appreciative reflection, grounded in the wisdom of appreciative inquiry, an individual or corporate practice that asks individuals to listen to our own and one another's stories of congregational and individual faith and life and then asks us to affirm, or "appreciate," the core spiritual values embedded in our stories.[4] Rather than looking for problems, visionary leadership, based on appreciative inquiry and reflection, looks for possibilities; rather than focusing on disease, this style of personal and corporate visionary leadership looks for signs of health; rather than denying death, visionary and appreciative leadership looks for fragile seeds of resurrection. Visionary pastors live by Dag Hammarskjold's affirmation:

For all that has been—Thanks!
To all that shall be—Yes![5]

The spirituality of visionary and appreciative leadership challenges us to listen for possibilities in even the most deadly or contentious congregational meeting. It seeks not to manage conflict but to transform it by recognizing that conflict is often a matter of having two very different, and possibly valuable, ideas discussed at the same time. Rather than imposing a vision from the outside, it invites people and the congregation as a whole to live in the interplay of memory and hope, tradition and innovation, by remembering those moments in which the congregation was most faithful, in which the movements of the spirit were palpable, and in which members felt energized and inspired. In times of congregational conflict, a third compromise option can always be hatched by affirmative leadership or, better still, many other even more innovative and creative options may emerge, if one does not at the outset see the two conflicting options as polarized and therefore to be defended.

Appreciative spiritual leadership always seeks to build the future on the best and the brightest, the most spiritually energizing achievements of the past, whether personal or corporate. But if pastors commit themselves to listening for their congregations' hopes and dreams, they must, first of all, take time to center themselves in their own sense of vocation. Appreciative inquiry and reflection as a path of visionary leadership can be a personal as well as an organizational practice in which pastors look for their moments of joy and vitality in their own ministries and, then, articulate their own vocational visions for the future in light of God's evolving work in their lives (Phil. 1:3–11).

As you look at your current ministry setting, you may choose to reflect on the following questions: Where do you find your greatest joy and vitality? What ministerial encounters have been most transforming for you and your congregation? As you consider your experiences of joy, vitality, and transformation, what spiritual values do you lift up as important in your ministry? Where is God calling you to move forward because of these spiritual values?

As a result of their own self-awareness, visionary leaders lead by listening rather than talking. When we have a clear sense of mission, grounded in our own pastoral discernment, we can better listen for images of mission and vision in the lives of others. When we are tempted to cling to our own vision as the truest manifestation of God's purposes for our congregations, we pastors are challenged to take a moment to *pause, notice, open, yield and stretch*, and then, based on what we have seen and heard, *respond* by reflecting before the congregation its polestar and guiding light, God's evolving vision. This spirit of appreciation and hope is reflected in a spirituality of pastoral trust and responsibility. Trusting God's wellspring of possibility, "the wise leader does not push to make things happen, but allows the process to unfold on its own." Accordingly, the spirit-centered leader "does not insist that things come out in a certain way."[6] Holistic spiritual leadership nurtures an environment of shared power and authority.

We pastors often fail to recognize that as leaders we are constantly exerting power in our attempts to guide our congregations. At issue, then, is the question, Will my use of power bring healing and wholeness and encourage people to find their own vocations in the body of Christ, or will my use of power be divisive and stand in the way of congregants' discovery and embodiment of God's vision for their lives and the congregation? Sadly, many pastors succumb to the temptation to lead "from above" by coercion rather than compassionate, appreciative, and imaginative listening and creativity. Coercive and unilateral leadership assumes that the pastor is the primary conduit for divine revelation in the congregation and that the pastor alone knows how to achieve God's vision for their church.

Bruce's Claremont (CA) Graduate School professor Bernard Loomer described coercive power as linear and unilateral in character. According to Loomer, the aim of linear or unilateral power is "to create the largest effect on the other while being minimally influenced by the other."[7] When pastors utilize linear and coercive power and frame conflicts in terms of the polarities good and evil, right and wrong, and win and lose, destructive resistance is inevitable. Such leadership forgets that spiritual leadership in the postmodern world involves claiming God's abundant revelation throughout a vast multifactorial network of people and influences, not the least of which is the congregation. Though seeking to listen appreciatively to God's voice in the many voices of the congregation and the world is often arduous and requires patience, you will discover that divine revelation whispers in the voices of the "least of these," including those who resist us, and in your own clearly articulated vision.

In contrast to unilateral and dominating approaches to leadership and power, the vision of spiritual leadership the two of us suggest focuses on power through relationship and compassion. According to Loomer, relational power involves

> *our openness to be influenced by another, without losing our identity.... [The use of relational power] is not only an acknowledgement and affirmation of the other as an end rather than a means to an end. It is also a measure of our own strength and size, even and especially when this influence of the other helps to effect a creative transformation of ourselves and our world.*[8]

In trusting God's revealing presence and vision for the future within the myriad voices in our congregations, we don't need to control administrative planning sessions. All we need to do is simply to be attentive to God's presence in our congregation as a whole and in the lives of congregants individually. In attending to God's many voices in the congregation, especially congregants' most energizing and inspiring experiences within congregational life and their personal and corporate dreams for the future, relationally centered pastors are more able to help the congregation discover the divine possibilities that emerge in the congregation's present as well as its future.

Compassionate leadership, even in the midst of conflict, does not demonize or polarize adversaries. Rather, the pastor holds to her evolving vision of God's presence in her congregation while maintaining close contact with her antagonists as well as her supporters. Spiritually centered ministerial self-differentiation opens, rather than closes, the pastor to those people whose visions differ from her own. While we don't deny the reality of clergy killers, that is, people who consistently and pathologically undermine spiritual leaders, compassionate spiritual leadership experiences the holy even in those people whose dysfunctional behavior contributes to congregational conflict and disease.[9] Even as they confront, and gather a team of trusted congregants and professionals to respond to such people, compassionate spiritual leaders still look for God's transforming presence in their congregants' lives. In the spirit of appreciative inquiry and reflection, they listen for the fears and hopes of their adversaries even as they seek to guide them toward God's emerging, and never fully embodied, vision for the church.

Cathy learned the meaning of spiritual leadership during a time in which her congregation erupted in conflict over the decision to make a public statement of welcome to people who are lesbian, gay, transgendered, or bisexual. After several months of study, employing a combination of Bible study, theological reflection, appreciative reflection, and spiritual visioning, the congregation was poised to make its public statement. Although she had come from a conservative religious background, Cathy became convinced by both Scripture and prayer that God loved people of all gender identities and that her calling was to nurture a congregation hospitable toward all people. In the course of the congregation's sacred conversations related to sexuality, she gently revealed her own position, not as the *only* response or the absolute authority in the congregation but as part of her own appreciative reflection on her own journey of faith. She saw her task as helping the church discern whether hospitality toward all people, including the LGBTQ community reflected God's vision for their congregation at this time. Still, a small contingency in the congregation resisted her vision and the vision of the majority of its membership. Presuming a linear, coercive model of pastoral leadership, they held her accountable for the church's decision-making process and asked her to resign.

Cathy admits that she was initially frightened and defensive when she was confronted by the threat of termination. She was tempted to use her pastoral authority to defeat the opposition; however, she chose another path: the path of relationship and compassion, grounded in the power of prayer and self-awareness. She looked for Christ's presence in her detractors even as she rallied support for her self-differentiated yet companioning role as a visionary spiritual leader. She sought to transform any attempt to polarize the factions in the congregation by responding directly and compassionately to people on each side. She held her ground personally and maintained her commitment to the vision of the congregation as a house for all peoples, but she also reached out to her opposition in friendship rather than enmity.

Affirmative, appreciative yet self-differentiating, visionary leadership can be stressful. Still, spiritual practices can keep us centered amid conflict. As she recalls, "Every time I was tempted to lash out at the opposition, I took several deep breaths and asked for God's guidance in being faithful to my calling for this church. When I felt myself losing my spiritual center and becoming anxious, I reminded myself that God had called me to this church and that however things worked out, God was with me and the congregation. I believed in the vision of radical hospitality and I trusted that regardless of the outcome, I would be faithful to my calling as pastor of this congregation." Cathy notes that she "protected the congregation's vision by reminding the leadership that the commitment to becoming open and affirming must be sincere if the congregation is truly to be a place of welcome." She also reminded them to be "hospitable to those who opposed the church's open and affirming hospitality." Cathy recalls telling her congregation that "Christians who have misgivings about homosexuality are not necessarily homophobic but rather have cultural, personal, or biblical reasons for their more conservative stance. We must remember that we are all persons of faith and commitment, despite our differences."

Ultimately, the congregation voted to become open and affirming of the LGBTQ community. While several members who opposed the decision left the congregation, the majority of them remained and chose to embrace the congregation's emerging patterns of hospitality. Cathy was grateful for God's presence and inspiration when one of the members of the group that had asked for her resignation apologized with the words, "This conflict could have split the church. I did not agree with your vision, and still am not fully there, but I trusted your compassionate leadership. I knew that you cared for me. You reached out and you listened. You held your own, but you allowed me the right to disagree. Today, I'm glad to call you my pastor." Appreciative, affirmative, visionary leadership follows the Benedictine spirit that we greet every congregant as if he or she were Christ.

Visionary leaders see God in all things and all things in God. Open to the creative movements of God in their lives and in the world, visionary pastors expect much of God and much of themselves and their congregations. As the pastor of a struggling United Church of Christ congregation noted, "I lived by scarcity and fear until I really encountered the Jesus of the Gospels. While I can't explain Jesus's healings or his welcome of people from every social class and place in society, I have come to believe that Jesus saw something of beauty in everyone, and I can do that as well. Jesus's table fellowship demonstrated his belief that God will provide for all of us and that God wants us to live abundantly. When I began to live by a bigger imagination, asking God to show me God's dream for my congregation and my ministry, I had new confidence that a way would be made through the congregation's wilderness. Our church is still struggling, but I believe God is at work here, and we're no longer afraid to explore new ways of doing things. Though we haven't grown much numerically, I feel a new spirit here—a spirit of trust, hope, and optimism."

Forward looking, appreciative, affirmative, and visionary leaders take time each day to imagine the new thing God is imagining for their lives and congregations. We don't worry so much about our individual dreams coming true because we trust that our faithful partnership with God in the concrete details of our ministries is part of something greater than we can imagine—God is incarnate in potluck dinners, in prayers with a dying elder, and in transformed minds in church school classes. God who began a good work in our lives and ministries will bring God's work to fullness, and it will be a "harvest of righteousness" (Phil. 1:11).

Management and Mysticism

The words of the little-known prophet Habakkuk provide a spiritual bridge that joins appreciative, affirmative, visionary leadership, and mystical management: "Write the vision; make it plain on tablets" (Hab. 2:2). Most pastors feel comfortable in the realm of theological imagination when they are teaching and preaching but not as comfortable with visionary leadership applied to church administration. A sense of God's presence and the call to share that presence with others in worship, teaching, prayer, and healing is what inspires many pastors to go into ministry. Many pastors are intrigued by the mysteries of faith and theological reflection and want others to experience their excitement about the quest to understand God and the world in which we live. Most pastors also believe that ministry is primarily about the big-picture issues of life, matters of life and death, justice and faithfulness, theology and personal growth. In light of this, many pastors believe that authentic ministry occurs primarily when they are called to share in others' moments of transformation and healing. They have difficulty experiencing God's spirit in the quotidian details of budgets, building management, and personnel supervision.

The two of us personally identify with the big-picture orientation in ministry. Bruce is, first and foremost, a teacher and administrator, but he is also a spiritual guide and healing companion. His greatest joys in ministry come from sharing the good news of divine transformation through writing, preaching, teaching theology, spiritual conversations, and healing encounters and from designing creative long-term programs for the seminary. As a pastoral caregiver, spiritual director, and church consultant, Kate finds her greatest joys in ministry when she is nurturing and guiding ministers and laypeople who are facing life-threatening illnesses and who are committed to holistic spiritual transformation. She feels her calling most clearly when she has the opportunity to be a resourceful partner to others in times of personal breakthrough. Yet, our experiences as pastors during the past thirty years tell us that ministry is also a matter of bricks and mortar and budgets and bottom lines as well as moments of personal and congregational transformation. In fact, the two of us have come to believe that nowhere is the Word of God more fully made flesh, disguised though it may be, than in board meetings, strategic planning sessions, personnel management, and budget sessions. Here, too, pastors must be trustworthy, faithful, and skilled. The way pastors incorporate their spiritual practices in response to the mundane aspects of ministry, in fact, determines the quality of their overall spirituality and effectiveness.

Still, congregational administration and management is the aspect of ministry that most easily takes pastors from the heights of personal theological reflection and spiritual centeredness to the depths of congregational chaos and confusion. Suzanne, an experienced pastor of a midsized American Baptist congregation, knows the challenges of maintaining her spiritual equilibrium as she undertakes the managerial and administrative responsibilities of ministry. "I'm sure glad I begin my day with a time of prayer and devotional reading. Those daily practices, along with a morning walk and a light breakfast, help me start the day feeling a sense of God's nearness. But, oh, how my life changes when I arrive at the church office each morning. My secretary greets me with the congregational 'crisis of the day.' Then, when I check my e-mail, it doesn't get any better. It seems my congregation is online 24/7 with some pressing complaint or concern. And, this is just an ordinary day."

Vital and spiritually centered pastors know that the rhythm of effective and faithful ministry involves integrating traditional pastoral practices of prayer and contemplation with their public duties of preaching, teaching, and worship leadership. Yet, often a spiritual cutoff occurs when pastors are faced with the professional organizational practices of building management, financial accountability, volunteer supervision, and personnel coordination. A veteran of more than a decade of faithful ministry in the United Methodist Church, Jason admits, "When I graduated from seminary, I never realized how many skills a pastor must utilize in the course of the day, sometimes one right after the other. Sometimes the multitasking makes my head spin and I need to slow down for a moment before I go to the next ministerial task. In the course of a day, I can spend an hour with a plumber, then drive to a nursing home for a pastoral visit, comfort a grieving widow, consult with youth group officers about the upcoming retreat, plan Sunday's service, and look over the church budget preparation for an evening board meeting. If I don't take a few minutes to pray every hour or so, I'll get so wound up in the tasks of ministry that I won't be able to be a pastor to my congregation." Susan and Jason are learning to live by the wise counsel attributed to Martin Luther: "I am so busy, that unless I pray four hours a day, I can't get my work done!"

In the following paragraphs, we will invite you to explore the spiritual dimensions of congregational administration and management. A spirituality of management, grounded in appreciative and affirmative reflection, is essential for today's pastors, given that congregational change is inevitable and failure to see God in the details, relationships, and decision processes of managing a church can only result in chaos. The two of us believe that spirit-centered and affirmative managers are (1) contemplative in their managerial style, (2) recognize that we are part of a dynamic body of Christ that holds many gifts and visions beyond our own, (3) place a high priority on encouragement and affirmation in their managerial relationships, and (4) expect and look forward to surprises as opportunities for creative transformation for themselves and their congregations. To those who ask, What's management got to do with ministry? prayerful pastors understand that their approach to management and administration is essential to their spiritual growth and the spiritual growth of their congregations.

Prayerful Management

Unless a pastor prayerfully walks through his day, he will most likely miss God's presence in the small details essential to faithful and inspiring management and administration. Indeed, in the ideal, our busiest days should be the most prayerful days. As an ardent follower of the practice of walking prayer, Bruce was delighted by Tom Peters's description of administration as "managing by wandering around."[10] Earlier in this text, we noted that a spiritual director is called to be "all eye." We believe the same wisdom applies to the mysticism of management. A spirit-centered manager is guided by prayerful attentiveness and appreciative reflection as he walks the hallways of the church building, visits nursing homes, participates in meetings, and interacts with staff, board members, and volunteers. Along with the pastoral imagination, cited as essential by Craig Dykstra, senior vice president for religion at the Lilly Endowment, we affirm the importance of prayerful observation. Spirit-centered pastors not only see the world through the eyes of their pastoral vocation but they also are attuned through their senses to the various currents of emotion, energy, commitment, and care in their congregation. They take time to notice prayerfully the dynamics in the church office, the state of the building, and the quality of congregational morale. They are both heavenly minded and earthly oriented.

Spirit-centered pastors join the quiet introversion of contemplation with the extroversion of action, described as "praying with your eyes open." A commitment to praying ministry's administrative details and practical concerns invites pastors to *pause, notice,* and *open* not only to God's presence in their inner lives, study, and spiritual and pastoral care but also to God's movements in the bricks and mortar of congregational life.

Now, we must admit that such prayerful and appreciative administration and management is not easy. Every pastor eventually recognizes the old adage that congregational leadership in the area of administration is much like herding feral cats. Chaos rather than order often characterizes the administrative life of the church. While congregants often blame pastors when things go wrong during the coffee hour or a church program, pastors are often scrambling up to the last minute to insure that the bathrooms are clean, doors unlocked, or supplies available. How on earth can we experience God's presence, in the spirit of Brother Lawrence, in the pots and pans and bricks and mortar of ministry, when trusted lay leaders fail to come through in providing the necessities for congregational operation, much less excellence? Amid the chaos of congregational life, every healthy pastor must live by twin mottos, the Serenity Prayer and Murphy's Law, if he or she is to embrace imperfection as the foundation for spiritual transformation.

As a seminary administrator depending on the support of other seminary departments for the quality of his programming, Bruce has learned to pray with his eyes open during the many, varied lifelong learning events that his department sponsors. As he manages by wandering around the seminary campus, he prayerfully notices the emotional and relational temperature of his staff; he checks for safety, security, and clean-liness on the seminary grounds; he observes the interactions of program participants; and he checks in with other depart-ments with whom he needs to work in order to insure high quality and hospitable programming. At times he has to take a deep prayerful breath before picking up the phone to get im-mediate action when another department has failed to provide materials or infrastructure for his programming.

In a similar fashion, Mary, a recently ordained Disciples of Christ pastor, has learned to take the spiritual temperature of her congregation by wandering about the church building. As Mary notes, "When I first arrive at church, I walk *around* the church building, prayerfully noting the condition of the prop-erty. Then, I walk *through* the building, looking at the condi-tion of restrooms and classrooms. When I walk *into* the office, I sit for a few minutes, especially on Mondays, and say a prayer with the church secretary before we look at the schedule of the week." Later, when she retreats to her study, Mary takes time to review the week ahead prayerfully. Mary integrates the forest and trees of ministry as she reflects on the week as a whole, not-ing her priorities, and then breaks the week down into discrete activities, both optional and necessary, for her faithful practice of ministry. According to Mary, "I no longer dread Monday mornings. If I take time to pray my schedule, I see the busiest weeks, even those with lots of meetings, as an opportunity to do God's will in various places. I have more than enough to do, but I don't feel rushed anymore. I know that God will give me what I need to get through the week with grace and care."

Mary embodies a Benedictine approach to management in which no deed is too small or too large to be an opportunity to serve God. Managing the tasks of ministry, from person-nel to building maintenance, becomes an opportunity for spiri-tual growth and pastoral care when pastors pray the tasks of their days. As we noted earlier, a pastor can breathe deeply and prayerfully as she goes from one task to another, reminding herself that all moments are holy moments and opening herself to God's guidance in every ministerial situation.

Such prayerful attentiveness is a pastor's greatest spiritual protection against the chaos of congregational life. As much as pastors aim at excellence in congregational hospitality reflected in well-kept buildings, safe environments, and clean restrooms, eventually they realize that their quest for congregational excellence depends on the faithfulness and cooperation of volunteers in church boards and committees. When things go wrong and necessary tasks are left undone as a result of neglect, pastors may have to spring into action, but they also need to let go of their need to be in control and awaken to God's presence, even in the inconveniences and imperfections of congregational life. We pastors must recognize the importance of prayerfully challenging as well as accepting imperfection as part of our spiritual growth. We prepare for administrative and management bumps not only through programmatic attentiveness and pastoral assertiveness but also through a life of prayerful openness to Christ's presence even in the most irresponsible board member.

John's attitude toward church board meetings was transformed when he began to pray the agenda. John confesses, "I used to dread the church session [board] meetings. They often were uninspired, unfocused, and frankly unnecessary, at least that was my attitude until I realized that the session meeting could be an opportunity for spiritual growth for myself and the session members. Initially, I began to pray about the items on the agenda. I noticed that my attitude changed. I took a chance and invited the church session to pray with me, not just a perfunctory prayer to get us started, but a time of silence and then prayerful noting of each item on the agenda. Together, we realized that budgets, personnel, and building issues reflected our mission to be a faithful community of faith and that our meetings were part of that mission."

The two of us have found, much to our amazement, that when a pastor moves from an attitude of dread or resistance to an attitude of prayer, the whole tenor of certain meetings and programs changes. Time and again, we have discovered the power of a transformed mind to change the atmosphere of meetings, staffs, and congregations. When pastors surround the details of ministry in prayer, we awaken to God's abundant life and God's wellspring of guidance and inspiration in those details. No longer living by fear and scarcity, we experience possibilities for personal transformation and pastoral care in every situation. When we choose to be attentive to God's presence in the details of our daily schedule or a meeting agenda, we can discover God actively present in the maintenance of a building, preparation for a meeting, dealing with staff conflicts, or working out the fine points of the treasurer's report. In the immediate moment, this may mean pausing to breathe deeply the spirit of God or quietly chanting the Jesus Prayer, "Lord, have mercy upon us," in the midst of a chaotic board meeting. It may mean when you are tempted to lash out at a contentious board member, excusing yourself from the meeting to take a moment for prayer. When you feel under attack or anxious about the congregation's financial condition in the course of a meeting, it may mean taking a second to imaginatively surround yourself in God's protective light, remembering that nothing can separate you from the love of God in Christ Jesus (Rom. 8:38–39).

Spiritual Bodywork

Experiencing the presence of God in a healthy and vital way throughout your ministry involves the dynamic interplay of *vision, promise,* and *practice.* Our theological vision gives shape to the ministry practices that enable us to fulfill the promise of discovering God's presence in our personal and professional lives. Central to a mystical approach to management is living by the uniting vision of the body of Christ and its dynamic interconnectedness (1 Cor. 12:4–31; Eph. 4:4–7, 11–16). Take a moment to recall Paul's appreciative and affirming words as your guide to life-giving, effective, and appreciative congregational administration in this spirit:

> Now there are varieties of gifts, but the same Spirit; and there are
> varieties of services but the same [God]; and there are varieties of
> activities, but it is the same God who activates all of them in every-
> one. To each is given the manifestation of the Spirit for the common
> good (1 Cor. 12:4–7).

Spiritually centered appreciative administration and management involves discovering, bringing forth, and trusting the many gifts present in the members of the congregation and in the congregation as a spiritual whole that is greater than the sum of its parts. First, spiritually affirmative and appreciative management, like all the other acts of ministry, reflects the synergy of theological vision and spiritual practice, grounded in recognizing God's dynamic presence in all things. If God is truly actively inspiring every member of your congregation, regardless of her or his current experience of God or physical, emotional, or mental health, then the insightful pastor looks for God's gifts in each person as a member of the body of Christ. The spiritually centered and affirmative pastor recognizes that each person in the congregation has many vocations and graces and that congregational vitality is advanced by helping parishioners learn to discover and share their gifts for the well-being of the whole.

The two of us recognize that maintaining a vision of God's presence in all people is difficult and sometimes virtually impossible in relationship to people whose behavior or mental health disrupts congregational life and challenges legitimate and ethically sound pastoral leadership. While we pastors may not be able to fix these situations, we can protect our pastoral integrity and spiritual leadership by nurturing our spiritual lives on a regular basis, especially in terms of our immediate responses to disruptive behavior patterns. In responding to difficult and disruptive people, the two of us suggest that you take a moment to breathe deeply, centering yourself in God's presence, and then repeat affirmations such as "God is with me and will protect me in this situation" or "Nothing can separate me from the love of God." The two of us also practice the Celtic *caim*, or "encircling," in such situations. Simply imagine yourself in a circle of divine protection as you repeat affirmations such as "God's circle surrounds and protects me" or "God is with me in this situation."

We recognize that maintaining the vision of God's presence and giftedness in the concreteness of congregational life in all its wonder as well as its imperfection is a tremendous challenge for pastors. Nevertheless, we send this challenge forth. When a pastor devotes herself to affirming God's presence in her congregants, regardless of their faults or limitations, her approach to ministry and management is transformed. A Presbyterian pastor in midlife, Judy has discovered what it means to see her management in terms of the body of Christ. She notes, "Each day when I come to church, I take a moment to collect myself before I get out of my car. I pray for the ability to see Christ in the church secretary, the sexton, and everyone who walks in the door. I monitor myself throughout the day and say an affirmative prayer to maintain my focus. My words are simple, and not very deep, just 'I see Christ in each one and help them see Christ in themselves.'"

Judy admits that this sort of affirmative appreciation is difficult, especially when she is in the midst of a challenging task. Judy confesses that "I want my church to be effective as an organization, and there are times when I find myself putting tasks ahead the people. Sometimes when I go home at the end of the day, I ask myself if I really saw them for who they are rather than what I want I want them to be and what I want to achieve for this church. I ask God for forgiveness and start all over again the next day." As Judy's experience notes, the key is intentional pastoral mindfulness in which we more regularly *pause, notice, and appreciatively yield* to God's presence in congregants before we assume to know God's calling for them and for ourselves.

Like most pastors, Judy recognizes that she can unconsciously fall into objectifying or manipulating her parishioners during a committee meeting or when she is trying to complete a project. At such moments, she remembers Jesus's attentiveness to unexpected interruptions and "unimportant" people. When she feels herself losing touch with the holiness of her parishioners, she returns to her simple practice, "I take a deep breath, ask for Christ's vision, and then repeat another simple affirmation, 'I am on holy ground. God is present in this person and this situation.'"

Management within the body of Christ involves affirming each person's gifts and each relationship within the body of Christ and helping each one live out her or his gifts in ways that bring vitality and health to themselves and the congregation. As Paul notes in Ephesians 4:11–13, God called some people to be "pastors and teachers, to equip the saints for the work of ministry, for building up the body of Christ, until all of us come to the unity of the faith and the knowledge of the Son of God, to maturity, to the measure of the full stature of Christ."

Most pastors are all too aware of their congregations' imperfections and their own very real limitations. Still, we believe that pastors can also experience the abundance of divine revelation in every life, including their own lives as pastors. Indeed, as we pastors commit ourselves to seeing God's gifts in our own lives, we can more readily discover God's vision of congregants' gifts. Our own sense of God's giftedness in our lives enables us to equip and empower others to see and live by their own gifts. Whether we pastor numerically growing or numerically declining congregations, we can experience grace, wonder, and surprise throughout the many tasks of ministry.

Management by Affirmation

Spiritual bodywork involves seeing the presence of God in the many gifted people who make up the body of Christ in your congregation and across the globe. Thus far, the two of us have stated that seeing the presence of God in the lives of congregants involves both vision and imagination through appreciative reflected and affirmative spiritual practices, grounded in awareness of our gifts in equipping ministry. Simply noticing the gifts of others is not enough. Spirit-centered pastors seek to appreciatively affirm God's presence in the congregation in both word and deed.

To use the language of attitudinal healing, spirit-centered pastors are love finders rather than fault finders; they affirm health rather than sickness, light rather than darkness, and abundance rather than scarcity.[11] Affirmative spiritual management appreciates God's graces in the congregation as a whole and individually in congregational staff, lay leaders, and volunteers and then regularly affirms their spiritual gifts and graces. Affirmative and appreciative management is characterized by words of gratitude, praise, and support. We believe that this attitude was at the heart of Jesus's quest for abundant life. For example, Jesus affirmed his disciples with these words, "You are the light of the world" (Matt. 5:14). With John's Gospel, we affirm that that God's light shines in everyone (John 1:9). In Jesus's ministry of affirmation, he saw a feast in a young boy's loaves and fishes; faithful leadership in Peter's ambivalence; generosity in Zacchaeus's dishonesty; purity in a woman's act of anointing; and charity in Martha's anxiety over meal preparations. We believe that Jesus was able to affirm others' giftedness because he first experienced himself as God's beloved son, commissioned to bring healing to the world.

Therefore, like detectives, pastors are called to search out the gifts in others' lives, tell the truth about them, and create a nurturing environment in which these previously unseen gifts can flourish and grow for the well-being of people and the community. We pastors honor and nurture the gifts of others by making frequent affirmative statements. Sharing the good news of God's gifts in people's lives both heals and empowers them, especially when their self-image has been shaped by negative comments by others or negative or limiting self-talk. In accenting the gifts and talents of others, the pastor becomes a midwife of divine possibility and hope.

The affirmative and appreciative manager might begin meetings with scriptural affirmations such as "You are the body of Christ," "You are the light of the world," or "God is working in your lives and in this church." Such affirmations are a prelude to affirming the gifts and successes of the congregation in order to provide perspective for discussing course corrections or more effective ways of embodying the congregation's mission. A Disciples of Christ pastor now beginning her fourth decade of ministry, Sarah remembers her initial surprise when her pastor told her following her graduation from college, "You have a gift for ministry. Why don't you consider enrolling in seminary?" "Before that time," Sarah confesses "I never realized a woman could pastor a church. But my pastor, a middle-aged male, not only urged me to consider seminary but also volunteered to drive me to my admissions appointment." Affirmations open new possibilities and awaken people to God's movements in their lives.

An affirmative and appreciative pastor takes time to notice and then affirm with others the gifts and graces he notices in their lives. Expressions of affirmation or gratitude are so simple that we often forget them. We can create an affirmative environment by using reality-based phrases such as "I'm grateful for your faithful work at the church. I see God's presence in the quality of office administration and hospitality" or "Thank you for your leadership in the board meeting. You're an effective and collegial leader" or "I'm grateful for your leadership in the youth group. I can see God's love in the way you relate to the teenagers."

As we stated earlier, we believe that practicing affirmative management begins with the pastor's own healthy self-affirmation. Healthy, spirit-centered pastors recognize that acknowledging and developing our own gifts is an expression of gratitude to God and to our own personal mentors. As Jesus counseled, we are called to let our light shine as a witness to God's love. Pausing to look at your life, what gifts do you notice in your daily life or hidden beneath the surface just waiting to be discovered and developed? Remember, you don't have to be perfect in order affirm your own giftedness. A Presbyterian pastor, Ray, takes a moment prior to each sermon to recite to himself the following affirmation: "God is working in my life, and my words will bring insight and healing to my congregation." A United Church of Christ pastor, Barbara, speaks a similar affirmation prior to congregational board meetings: "With God as my inspiration, my words will be wise and my responses insightful." During a time of congregational conflict, David remembers constantly affirming, "I am a strong and centered leader. Nothing can separate me from the love of God."

Remembered and repeated over and over again, such affirmations transform our minds and our ministries and open us to recognize and empower our congregations. In liberating us from self-limitation, affirmations bring forth possibilities for pastors, parishioners, and congregations. As you look at your ministry, what words of affirmation do you need to hear from God? What affirmations do you need to recite to yourself in your own quest for wholeness? What affirmations do you need to speak to your colleagues, staff members, or parishioners? What particular affirmations might challenge and transform attitudinal limitations in your congregation?[12] Affirmative and appreciative pastoral administration is not Pollyannaish in style but rather insightful in perception, noting realistic achievements, faithful service, and positive growth wherever it occurs. Affirmative and appreciative pastoral administration creates a healing and supportive environment in which people can achieve excellence in their congregational roles without guilt or fear of failure.

Embracing the Unexpected

Amelie, the associate pastor of a large suburban United Church of Christ congregation recognizes that good pastors must creatively embrace surprise. She notes, "You never know what's going to happen when you pick up the phone. Just one call can change your whole week." Matt, another associate pastor, adds, "I recognized that I need to expect the unexpected. When I think I can fully manage my work, I miss what's most important in ministry, having a plan but being willing to drop everything to respond to God's call. Some weeks, God's unexpected call comes through the death of a long-time member; other weeks, it comes through having to manage a youth retreat or building maintenance problem. I've discovered that when I embrace surprise, I feel most alive and intentional in my ministry."

Both of these pastors have captured the wisdom of Forrest Gump, cited earlier in this book: "Life is like a box of chocolates, you never know what you're gonna get." They have come to know that ministry, like time, can never be fully managed; but pastors can be intentional in integrating order and chaos, and structure and novelty, in their ministries. They have come to believe that while God may not decide the details of our lives, God is in the midst of every event, including and perhaps even most present in the unexpected events that rearrange our days and transform our lives.

A pastor who leads with a sense of wonder and appreciation for the unexpected must have a personal sense of vision and a flexible plan to guide his path; he must always be willing to modify his vision while dealing with the graceful chaos that characterizes much of ministry. The self-differentiated pastor, who knows himself and has a clear sense of God's presence and vision for his life and congregation, is always able to find his center within the surprising challenges of ministry. Spirit-centered ministry involves an evolving marriage between skillful ministerial practice and alignment with God's novel movements in the present moment.

Spirit-centered pastors can discern God's vision within the many surprising events of their ministries. While we do *not* attribute chaos, suffering, or failure to God's will, we nevertheless can envisage God seeking wholeness and order within the many diverse movements of life. We also recognize that divine creativity, embodied within a vision of abundant life and wholeness, is the source of both novelty and creative chaos, when we confront obsolete congregational practices, institutional idols, and unjust structures. Theologically speaking, if God's vision is dynamic, constantly adjusting to the realities of the world as God seeks wholeness in the most unlikely and difficult places, then alignment with God involves the same dynamic interplay of embodying your long-term vision amid the shifting realities of daily life.

Seeking to embrace order and chaos, regularity and surprise, one pastor notes, "I used to try to control what went on in church. Now I realize that the more I try to control the congregation, the more it will control my well-being and close me off to God's unexpected blessings. When I want things just so or have a plan that can't be modified, I'm at the mercy of every divergent opinion or unexpected event. But when I trust God in the flow of ministry, with both its surprising joy and unexpected pain and conflict, I experience a greater sense of peace and discover new ways of creatively responding to chaos. When everything falls apart and I have to shift from Plan A into Plan B or even to Plan C, I know that I will make it, and that I have the resources to respond to every crisis as long as I seek God's wisdom for that situation."

We have come to believe that agility in ministry, like agility in athletics, interpersonal relationships, or foreign policy, involves the lively interplay of vision, plan, preparation, skill, and openness to change. Appreciative and affirmative pastors embrace change as part of practicing the presence of God in ministry because they trust that God is faithfully active in every unexpected situation.

Once again, Gerald May's process of awareness provides a foundational spiritual practice for embracing change. When you receive the unexpected and challenging phone call or e-mail or when the copying machine breaks down as the Sunday bulletin is being printed, take a moment to *pause*. Unless it is an absolute emergency, take a few centering breaths, remember a spiritual affirmation, or walk around the block or down the hallway to the water fountain. *Notice* your initial response and briefly evaluate the problem at hand and its impact on the people around you, if you are in a group. *Open* to God's vision within the situation. In such situations, although we may not be able to discern God's vision with any clarity at the time, opening ourselves to God can awaken us to peace within the storm. Like Peter the disciple, when we open to God's presence and keep our eyes on Jesus, we can face the storm, even if we can't walk on water! In a split second, we can choose to *yield* and *stretch* into God's new possibilities, awakening us to a vision and hope greater than our own, knowing that God will supply the wisdom and sustenance we need. From this deeper wisdom and vision, we can discover a healing and calming *response* that brings peace to stressful situations. Embodying a nonanxious presence in ministry is not accidental but the gift of a long-term commitment to opening to God's transforming presence in every changing situation. God's love is surprising, and God's faithfulness is everlasting, embracing and inspiring us in every moment and in every change.

Practicing the Presence of God in Administration

While we pastors cannot manage either time or ministry, we *can* learn practices that make the many tasks of people and program administration a holy adventure, awakening us and our congregations to the transforming love of God.

Praying the Tasks of Ministry

Affirmative, appreciative, spiritually centered administration involves joining leadership with management in ministry. Effective pastors who maintain their spiritual center in the many tasks of administration can see God's presence in ministry's everyday details. Such centeredness allows them to recognize that congregational growth and vitality and ministerial effectiveness involve *how* they lead and manage just as much as *what* their congregation achieves. Moment by moment, pastors are called to join, hand in hand, commitment to developing their interpersonal communication and organizational leadership skills with appreciative and affirming prayerful awareness in which spiritual practices lead to holy and holistic habits of mind.

While there is no *one* path to praying the tasks of ministry, the two of us have found, once again, that the simple sequence of *pausing* and *noticing* and then *praying* as we move from one task to another is especially helpful in practicing the presence of God in our pastoral roles as leaders, managers, and administrators. We suggest that you begin by simply pausing to pray as you check your e-mail and write responses, or as you answer your office or cell phone. Expand this habit to include noticing your deepest feelings, thoughts, and body tensions as you arrive at your office or enter a church board meeting. You may choose, as we suggested in an earlier chapter, to say a prayer or take a deep centering breath as you enter a hospital room, begin a pastoral appointment, or prepare for a meeting. Although all of these prayers relate to and support the spiritual quality of your pastoral and administrative tasks, first and foremost they begin with care for your own spiritual well-being. The overall quality your own spiritual life moment by moment and over the long haul is the primary medium of your ministry as a pastor. Awareness of your mental, emotional, and spiritual well-being in the present moment is essential to authentic representation of God's presence with and for others. It also helps one prevent reactive and defensive behaviors in stressful administrative situations. Our stature and integrity as pastors depend on our openness to the whole of our experience of God's movements in our lives. Letting holistic spiritual self-care permeate your ministry involves reminding yourself that every ministerial task is an opportunity to deepen the spiritual lives of others as well as your own, and vice versa.

Affirmative Management

The two of us have experienced the power of affirmative faith to transform lives, liberate possibilities, and enable people to discover God's many gifts as members of the body of Christ and citizens of the world. Still, the two of us also recognize that compartmentalized understandings of congregational administration prevail. Pastors and lay leaders, who are schooled in the ways of secular business management, often separate matters of faith from matters of bricks and mortar and spirituality from budgets and personnel issues. It is our job as pastors to gently and affirmatively call them to encounter God in every administrative task. Helping others experience holiness in the tasks of leadership and management cannot be judgment based but must be grounded in affirmative words and actions. We must not only share the good news of grace by our words but also act gracefully, creating administrative environments that are safe, effective, and inspiring. This is often a challenging discipline. In this section, we seek to provide appreciative and affirmative resources that can heal and transform church staff and their workplaces and church boards and committees.

First of all, as affirmative pastors, we must begin with our own self-affirmation, which is not a matter of pride but recognizing God's presence and giftedness in your life. Can you imagine saying the following biblical affirmations throughout each day? Try one or two in the course of each day this week.

> I am the light of the world and I will let my light shine, so that God may be glorified (Matt. 5:14–16).
> I am God's beloved child (Matt. 3:17).
> God's light is constantly enlightening me (John 1:9).
> God gives me words of wisdom to share (Jer. 1:9).

Second, as affirmative pastors, we can discover these truths in our own lives, but we can also discover them in the lives of our congregants. For example, at an appropriate moment share one of the following affirmations with a congregant:

> God loves you; you are God's beloved child (John 3:16, Matt. 3:17).
> Jesus says you are the light of the world and you can bring light to this church and your family (Matt. 5:14–16).
> You are a gifted member of God's family (1 Cor. 12:7, 12).

Third, what would it be like for you, as an appreciative and affirmative pastor, to reassure yourself and your congregation in times of congregational challenge with words such as:

> Nothing can separate us from the love of God in Christ Jesus (Rom. 8:38–39).
> Wherever we are, God's spirit is sustaining us (Ps. 139:7–12).
> God will supply our deepest needs (Phil. 4:19).

Fourth, as you consider your own life as a pastor, which of the words of spiritual affirmation noted above do you need to hear and embrace in order to experience God's transforming love right now? Take time to immerse yourself in them. Repeat your biblical affirmation to yourself three or four times. Write it on a sticky note and on your bathroom mirror, refrigerator door, or daily calendar. Whenever you catch yourself reading the affirmation, pause and notice how you feel as you let the truth of the affirmation reverberate through your cares and concerns of the day. Take time to journal about what you discover. Expect surprises and expect to experience God's love and grace anew and, most important, plan to respond creatively to what you have experienced.

Fifth, as you consider your work as a pastor, what gifts and empowering words do you need to share with particular members of your congregation? What affirming words do you need to share with the congregation as a whole? This could be the most challenging aspect of practicing the appreciative spirituality we are suggesting, especially since many congregations live by an attitude of scarcity or they repeat over and over, in their language and organizational behavior, negative scripts and unhealthy responses to change.

In letting the light of appreciative spirituality shine, we suggest that you consider the spiritual equivalent of sticky notes in congregational newsletters and electronic communications. Without denying the challenges your congregation faces, share the good news and giftedness you are observing on a regular basis. While this will not solve every congregational problem, it will help your congregation experience its challenges from the perspective of abundant giftedness rather than fearful scarcity. Practicing congregational affirmation is especially powerful when joined with a corporate visioning process such as appreciative inquiry. (Of course, the two of us recognize the possibility that you as pastor may find it virtually impossible to recognize and affirm the gifts of your congregation, given its current situation. If this is the case, we believe that it is important for you to meet with a spiritual director and engage in a process of discernment by which you can holistically and prayerfully assess the fit between your gifts and personality and the issues facing the congregation.)

Appreciative and Affirmative Reflection in Ministry

Practicing the presence of God in both in your contemplative and public ministry is grounded in your recognition that God is always at work in your life, aiming at health and creative transformation in the present and the future. While the corporate process of appreciative inquiry as a visioning and strategic planning tool can transform congregational life in its integration of gratitude, vitality, and possibility, our goal in this text is your transformation as pastor so that you can be a more creative and effective partner in healing and transforming your congregation. Trusting God's gentle, affirmative movements toward wholeness throughout your life, you can practice appreciative and affirmative spiritual reflection in your ministry by following a flexible approach to this step-by-step process:

1. Remembering those life-giving moments in which you experienced God's presence in your life. (You might choose to recount this moment in your journal or by drawing a picture or making a collage.)
2. Remembering life-giving moments in ministry in which you felt fully alive in your ministerial tasks. (Again, take time to recount this moment on paper or in a work of art.)
3. Acknowledging what you most value about your life and ministry. Without being overly modest, take time to affirm God's giftedness embodied in your most vital and meaningful experiences in your life and ministry.
4. Take time to reflect on how you can build upon these vital, life-giving, and holy moments in your current life and ministry.

5. Reflecting on your experiences of vitality and meaning, write and or draw a picture of your future vision of wholeness and vitality in ministry.

6. Starting small, what immediate steps can you take to affirm this vision of reality and begin to realize its possibilities in your life and ministry? Reflect on how you might share these intentional steps with your congregation as it seeks to be faithful to its vision.

7. Last but not least, write a covenant of affirmative personal and professional transformation for yourself—that is, a promise to God that affirms and celebrates the practice of appreciative spiritual reflection you have just completed. Date your covenant and then commit yourself to prayerfully reflect and act upon it in your personal and professional life for a specific length of time.[13]

The two of us believe that appreciative and affirmative spiritual reflection join the personal and the professional, the private and the public, and the contemplative and the active aspects of ministry. Living by the spirit of appreciative reflection not only can deepen and transform pastors' attitudes toward congregational leadership and administration but also enable us to fulfill our roles as leaders and managers with vision, integrity, intentionality, and collegiality. In discovering our own vitality and meaning in life and ministry, we will more effectively inspire the congregations we lead to fulfill their roles as lively and mission-oriented members of the body of Christ.

Prophetic Hospitality

Pastor JoAnn came home from her Disciples of Christ church in a rage the Sunday after the 2008 Republican National Convention. Her first words to her husband after closing the door of the church parsonage were, "What's wrong with these clueless people? They're so excited about the Republican choices for president and vice president. It's like Jesus was coming again, the way they talk! I had to bite my tongue all through coffee hour as they extolled the virtues of the presidential candidate's running mate. What was worse is that they think I agree with them. Haven't they been hearing my sermons about the need to care for strangers and immigrants and welcome diversity in our community? I wanted to scream. What I am doing here in this church?"

We suspect that conversations like this occur regularly following worship and board meetings in many clergy households. Most of the mainstream pastors in our ministerial excellence groups note that a significant theological, political, and cultural gulf lies between them and their congregations. We have also observed a similar political and cultural dissonance present among a growing number of evangelical pastors, whose politics and mores, in the past, have traditionally been congruent with the ethics and political positions of their parishioners. Many evangelical pastors are now giving priority to environmental stewardship, as demonstrated by their preaching and by encouraging congregational social action, and are less concerned about the traditional political divides related to abortion and homosexuality.

After talking with several church leaders following a church board meeting, Steve, a self-described evangelical pastor of a Church of the Brethren congregation, drove home with a sense of despair at the church leaders' attitudes toward the most economically vulnerable members of their local community. Steve lamented, "For the past two years, I've been preaching about how a personal relationship with Jesus means living like Jesus, feeding the hungry, caring for children, reaching out to the lost. But the minute a few of us suggest that our church become part of the community soup kitchen or that our building be used as one of the sites of the winter homeless shelter, there's an uproar in the congregation. Some members think the poor are lazy and don't deserve our charity—after all 'The Lord helps those who help themselves.' Don't they read the Bible at all? Their faith seems to be all about individual responsibility and personal salvation. The condition of the fellowship hall carpet is more important to them than the condition of the homeless. I'd like to give all of them a tongue-lashing from the pulpit this Sunday! Haven't they ever read Matthew 25?"[1]

The two of us believe that pastoral ministry involves the interplay of challenge and companionship, sharing and silence, especially as it relates to the cultural and political divides of our time. Bruce recalls being caught by surprise when a parishioner of the country church where he was serving as interim pastor shared his reasons for not voting for a particular presidential political candidate. His congregant averred, "You know, if we elect a Democratic president, they'll take away our guns!"

Some church members express their political views openly in worship or committee meetings, while others forward vitriolic, politically biased, and factually inaccurate political e-mails to the congregation, assuming that their pastor and the rest of the church agrees with them. When such communications occur, and pastors realize the wide cultural and political gulf that separates them from congregants, some pastors simply give up the fight for nuanced reflection and dialogue and simply avoid preaching on topics that would stir up congregational conflict. Many hide their own belief systems in order to avoid discomfort, conflict, and dissention for themselves and their congregations. Although such strategies avoid overt conflict within the congregation, eventually such efforts sap such pastors of their theological and pastoral vitality, and threaten the integrity of their sense of call.

We have heard pastors keep their beliefs safely to themselves among their congregants, but then in the safety of collegial gatherings berate their congregants' ignorance. This ethical disconnect eventually leads to growing alienation and emotional distancing from the congregation. As one pastor noted, "I'm struggling right now. I'm having trouble being pastor of a congregation whose beliefs and values I can't respect. I can't relate to their excitement about the right to have prayer in schools or the inalienable right to bear arms. But what really bothers me is their silence and inaction about feeding the hungry or supporting our denomination's health care initiatives. When it comes to politics, we're on different planets! Maybe, I should think of going to a church where I can preach what I believe."

In such situations, the truth is that when pastors publicly get angry and denounce their congregants' political positions, they can lose their credibility as spiritual leaders within their congregations. Recently, Bruce heard the account of a Midwestern pastor who unexpectedly unleashed a shouting match during worship when he made an inept comparison between the Israelites worshiping the golden calf and his church having an American flag in the chancel of the sanctuary. In the wake of his remarks, some members called for the pastor's resignation, and you can be sure the flag still remains on the chancel!

The two of us have strong political and cultural viewpoints that reflect our progressive, open and affirming, and inclusive theological positions. We believe that pastors are called to be both prophets, who challenge the spiritual and cultural status quo in their communities, and shepherds, who comfort and nurture their congregations. Still, we know that as congregational pastors, we must learn to share our prophetic insights in ways that connect us with as well as challenge our congregations. To use the language of congregational systems theory, spiritually centered pastors can, and should, be prophetically self-differentiating as they share their theologically grounded visions of the congregation's responsibility to promote social justice, while nurturing intimately caring relationships with people in their congregations who hold differing political and social viewpoints.

In this chapter, we will reflect on ways we pastors can be both hospitable and prophetic in our diverse congregations and communities. How we pastors deal with political diversity in our congregations is crucial both to our own spiritual well-being and to the spiritual care of our congregations. Indeed, prophetic hospitality is one of the most difficult spiritual practices to pursue insofar as prophetic ministry and the call to reach out to the vulnerable can provoke anxiety and defensiveness among congregation members and their leaders. Pastors need to cultivate appreciative and affirmative reflection in order to maintain their own spiritual centers and pastoral integrity while seeing God's presence in those who resist their initiatives.

The Prophetic Ministry of the Pastor

We believe that personal and social transformation is at the heart of the church's mission. This vital interdependence was modeled by the One who ate with sinners, prostitutes, and tax collectors. As Jesus's followers, we are challenged to share the life-transforming social agenda that was central to the teachings and healing ministry of Jesus. Certain of his mission as the messenger of God's coming reign, Jesus saw his own prophetic ministry as embodying the prophetic heritage of Israel.

Quoting the prophet Isaiah, Jesus proclaimed, "The Spirit of the Lord is upon me, because he has anointed me to bring good news to the poor. He has sent me to proclaim release to the captives and recovery of sight to the blind, to let the oppressed go free; to proclaim the year of the Lord's favor" (Luke 4:18–19).

According to Mark's Gospel, in the wake of Jesus's baptism and the subsequent arrest of his spiritual companion John the Baptist, Jesus began his public ministry by proclaiming "the good news of God, and saying, 'The time is fulfilled, and the kingdom of God has come near; repent, and believe in the good news'" (Mark 1:14–15). New Testament theologian N. T. Wright describes Jesus as "a first century Jewish prophet," whose preaching of repentance called people to "give up their agendas and trust [God's agenda]."[2] Theologian and New Testament scholar Marcus Borg concurs with Wright by affirming that Jesus was a spiritual and social prophet of God's reign. According to Borg, Jesus presented a "compassionate, boundary shattering vision," which intimately joined spiritual transformation with social transformation as essential components of God's coming reign. According to Borg, "mystical experience leads not only to a different way of seeing God and the world, but also a different way of seeing people."[3] Mystical experiences invite us to both visualize and enact God's reign "on earth as it is in heaven." From Borg's perspective, Jesus's proclamation of God's reign intimately connects the roles of prophet and spirit person in both Jesus's ministry and in our own. The two of us believe that such a connection was the result of Jesus's attunement with God's presence in all of life that enabled him to see and, then, bring forth the light of the world in the most unexpected people and places.

In that same spirit, New Testament theologian John Dominic Crossan describes Jesus's table fellowship as the incarnation of God's reign of everyday life. Jesus's "kingdom of nobodies" stands in stark contrast to systems based on wealth, power, purity, and exclusion. According to Crossan, "the kingdom of God

is what the world would be like if God were directly and immediately in charge."[4] Jesus's radical message of hospitality included everyone, from a Samaritan leper and Roman centurion
to a rich young Jewish ruler and a daughter of Abraham caught
in adultery. Jesus's healing ministry, embodied in transforming
and boundary-breaking actions, reflects in the challenges of everyday life God's dream of healing communities and families *as
well as* bodies and spirits. We pastors can imagine God's realm,
paint pictures of it in our teaching and preaching and in our
pastoral care, and then do all we can to make God's reign come
on earth and in heaven. The Gospels portray Jesus in times of
conflict as never backing down theologically, relationally, or
ethically. Despite his controversial vision, Jesus sought to welcome all people as he lived out his vision of God's coming reign.
To be sure, Jesus was a pastor as well as a prophet, and we can
be too.

Jesus lived out an alternative vision of reality that Walter
Brueggemann has aptly described as a "prophetic imagination"
in which personal and corporate visionary spirituality lead to
words of protest and lamentation; and words of protest and
lamentation lead to social transformation. As Brueggemann
notes, "Prophetic ministry is identified with direct prophetic
encounter with established power," grounded in the prophet's
grief at the distance between God's vision for humankind and
the social and economic realities of injustice, exploitation, poverty, and neglect. The two of us stand with Brueggemann in
believing that "human transformation actively depends on a
transformed imagination."[5] A transformed imagination is ultimately the fruit of spiritual practices and the imaginative insights that emerge from them.

True to the message of Jesus and his prophetic predecessors, faithful, spirit-centered ministry is almost always at odds
in some way with the status quo in our congregations and communities because it always calls us forward into God's new creation. God hears the cries of the poor, and faithful pastors are

challenged to help their congregations become attuned to these same cries.

For the sake of congregants and the world, faithful pastors must present creative, biblically based alternatives to the popular self-centered prosperity theologies as well as the idolatries of nation and race. In contrast to many congregants' close identification between God and country, prophetic pastors are called to proclaim that "God so loved the world" (John 3:16), the whole world, not just the United States of America, and that God makes the "sun rise on the evil and on the good, and sends rain on the righteous and on the unrighteous" alike, both *within* and *beyond* our nation's borders (Matt. 5:45). While few mainstream and progressive pastors have the hubris to say, "Thus saith the Lord" at the conclusion of their most prophetic sermons, the majority of mainstream and progressive pastors clearly recognize that, for the most part, their congregations have adopted a complacent religion that congregants don't want disturbed, most especially by the Bible's prophetic vision. Few average churchgoers distinguish between American consumerism and promotion of military power, on the one hand, and the countercultural teachings of Jesus as healer and prophet, on the other. As one pastor notes, "When my congregants say the words 'God and country,' they really mean that America is God's chosen land, a city on a hill with a special destiny." In words reminiscent of the experience cited a few paragraphs above, he wonders, "If push comes to shove, it might be more difficult to remove the Christian flag than the communion table from the sanctuary." Under the circumstances, many pastors ask, "How can we teach and preach prophetically and biblically while staying in healthy communication with our congregants?"

Whether the focus involves issues of justice, economics, global warming, immigration, sexual abuse, health care, science, or violence and war, the ultimate challenge for those who seek to be pastors is to join challenge with compassion, vision with relationship, and theological distance with healthy relatedness.

As pastors we know that any questioning of the status quo in our congregations will stir up resistance and opposition among certain church members. Yet, if we are to preserve our integrity as pastors, we need to step forth with a prophetic voice in a way appropriate to our personality and context. Our answer is to embrace a creative vision of what the two of us call prophetic hospitality—that is, to engage in strong advocacy for the vulnerable, reflected in word and action, while at the same time encouraging equally strong expression and discussion of diverse social and political viewpoints in the congregation. The two of us see this approach as profoundly spiritual in nature, beginning with the pastor cultivating spiritual practices that enable her or him to see and appreciate Christ's presence both in the "least of these," the most vulnerable people in their communities, and also in the faces of all people within their politically and culturally diverse congregations.

Making Space for Diversity

Jesus was known for his prophetic hospitality. As the savior and healer of all people, Jesus scandalized friend and foe alike with his subversive hospitality. Consider the Gospel stories: Can you imagine Jesus's disciples' reaction when Jesus unexpectedly invited himself to lunch at the home of Zacchaeus, a Jewish tax collector viewed by his fellow citizens as a traitor who chose to exploit his own people for personal profit and security? Can you visualize Jairus's surprise when Jesus responded to his anguished plea without pointing out that Jairus, as the leader of the synagogue, no doubt suspected Jesus's religious orthodoxy? What do you suspect the "righteous ones" were thinking when Jesus stood beside a woman accused of committing adultery or when Jesus defended the generosity of a woman who anointed his feet with precious anointment? A few years later, imagine the scandal in the early Christian community when Philip related his baptism of an Ethiopian eunuch, whose sexual identity was condemned by Jewish law. Truly Jesus was the incarnation and the model for his first followers, as well as for us, of God's embrace of all people in the reign of God.

The first followers of the way of Jesus saw hospitality as a sign of the new creation they experienced in the days following the dramatic unleashing of God's Spirit at Pentecost. As Acts proclaims:

> Awe came on everyone, because many signs and wonders were being done by the apostles. All who believed were together and had all things in common; they would sell their possessions and goods and distribute the proceeds to all, as any had need. Day by day, as they spent much time together in the temple, they broke bread at home and ate their food with glad and generous hearts, praising God and having the goodwill of all the people (Acts 2:43–47).

Spirit-centered living for the first followers of Jesus led not only to a new experience and understanding of God's presence in their lives but also to transformed relationships and economic attitudes. This same life-transforming hospitality was at the heart of Paul's letter to the Galatians. Anguished and angered by the prospect of communities made up of first- and second-class Christians, the apostle Paul proclaims God's all-embracing and grace-filled welcome: "As many of you as were baptized into Christ have clothed yourself with Christ. There is no longer Jew or Greek, there is no longer slave or free, there is no longer male and female; for all of you are one in Christ Jesus" (Gal. 3:27–28).

In a century in which people's primary identity was defined by their social position, Paul asserts that in Christ the wall of separation between the various tribes of humankind has been broken. This same spirit is at work in Paul's words to the Christians in Corinth. Paul recognizes the many diverse spiritual and theological streams within the Corinthian church and the consequent danger that people will place their own theological positions ahead of their relationship with Christ and their fellow members of Christ's body. While Paul does not deny the wisdom present in differing streams of Christian theology and practice, he asserts that our unity in Christ relativizes every theological position, including his own, when he asks the Corinthians, "Has Christ been divided? Was Paul crucified for you? Or were you baptized in the name of Paul?" (1 Cor. 1:13). Like the differences many of today's pastors have with their colleagues and leaders, Paul had strong theological and ethical convictions that, on occasion, led to conflict with the apostle Peter and many of the leaders of the Jerusalem church. But in moments of personal self-transcendence, Paul also recognized that in Christ our theological treasures are contained in fallible and time-bound earthen vessels.

Amid cultural, sexual, liturgical, and theological wars that split congregations, provoke pastoral dismissals, and threaten the overall well-being of pastors and congregations, the spirit of hospitality is being reclaimed as an essential Christian practice. We believe that prophetic hospitality is at the heart of theological reflection, spiritual practice, and Christian ministry in the way of Jesus. According to Christian educator Delia Halverson, "Hospitality is a lifestyle rather than an act of culture... Hospitality is recognizing Christ in everyone and acting accordingly."[6] In a hospitable world, reflecting a hospitable God, no people or places are God-forsaken and no people are beyond transformation and reconciliation. To believe and affirm the traditional doctrine of divine omnipresence means that God is surely present in *every* life, however hidden that presence may be, always seeking to nurture healthy relationships, personal well-being, and ethical responsibility. Amy Oden, professor of church history at Wesley Theological Seminary adds, "God's hospitality is God's welcome into a new way of seeing and living." According to Oden, "Gospel hospitality is God's welcome into abundant life, where our welcome is rooted. Living in God's welcome, we experience the marks of readiness, risk, and recognition."[7]

The vision of hospitality the two of us affirm is profoundly prophetic in nature. Rather than dismissing, disregarding, or denying the insights of those with whom we pastors disagree theologically, politically, relationally, ethically, or liturgically, the prophetic spirit of hospitality challenges us to seek and appreciate God's presence in the most unlikely people and places. While some people more than others in our congregations and communities may demonstrate that they are attuned to God's movements in their lives and the world, the two of us assert that God plays no favorites. Regardless of their theological, ethical, or spiritual maturity or gifts, we believe that God is still working in all people's lives, inviting each of us to play our own unique role in God's realm of shalom, peace, and justice. God does not polarize but welcomes into God's realm those whom we might otherwise wish to forsake in the darkness of theological and political ignorance. As Jesus asserts: "You have heard that it was said, 'You shall love your neighbor and hate your enemy.' But I say to you, Love your enemies and pray for those who persecute you, so that you may be children of your [Parent] in heaven; for [God] makes [the] sun rise on the evil and on the good, and sends rain on the righteous and on the unrighteous" (Matt. 5:43–45).

These words convict progressive as well as conservative pastors when we are tempted to consider those who resist our viewpoints as utterly misguided or sinful. The God of Jesus is a God of abundant grace, who seeks the healing and transformation of all people and communities, who loves without limitation, and who calls us to embody that same theological and spiritual inclusiveness when we must challenge the prevailing mores and beliefs of our congregation, culture, or nation. The hard work of hospitality joins personal self-awareness, spiritual practices, and the pursuit of theological breadth as well as depth. It is a commitment to profound pastoral and theological self-differentiation through which we share our vision of God's realm in ways that reach out to our diverse congregants and community members. While holding before congregants God's vision of shalom and justice, which challenge every institution, including our own congregations, we are equally called to stay in relationship with those who challenge our own viewpoint and continue to hold firmly to polarizing political, ethical, and cultural judgments. Prophetic hospitality is grounded in a visionary reconciliation in which pastors see and appreciate Christ's presence in the all their congregants as the foundation of common ground amid great diversity. Still, as Amy Oden notes, "offering hospitality to the theological stranger does not mean that we must agree with that person's position or that we have to abandon our own."[8] It does mean, however, that we treat the "stranger" who opposes our theological, liturgical, and ethical values with the same respect and care that we give to those whose rights and values we are seeking to protect. While we may clearly challenge certain behaviors and viewpoints in our congregations, we must also remember that "unless we are open to hearing all opinions, we neglect hospitality."[9]

Similar to Cathy whose leadership spirituality in the area of welcoming gay and lesbian people was described in chapter 4, Stephanie found the path of prophetic hospitality life transforming and personally challenging when her congregation also sought to become a place of welcome for gay, lesbian, transgendered, and bisexual people. Although her concern for hospitality toward LGBTQ people was inspired by the concrete values of many members of her congregation, both gay and straight, Stephanie recalls being surprised at "some of the attitudes in my congregation toward the gay and lesbian, bisexual, and transgendered people who worshiped beside them. Some people saw my open hospitality to LGBTQ people and my support of the grassroots initiative to become an open and affirming congregation as a turning away from Scripture. That made me angry at first, and I was tempted to condemn them publicly." But Stephanie listened to a deeper spiritual wisdom inspired by conversations with her spiritual director that enabled her to see her opponents as God's beloved children too.

About the time her congregation was considering becoming publicly open and supportive of the LGBTQ community, Stephanie encountered a group called Silent Witness at a rally for LGBTQ rights. Silent Witness seeks to "provide a non-confrontational buffer between those who condemn others based on their sexual orientation or identity and those they condemn."[10] The work of Silent Witness reminded Stephanie of the nonviolent work of Mahatma Gandhi, Martin Luther King Jr., and Desmond Tutu. Convicted by her own anger at those who resisted a welcoming theology, Stephanie committed herself to become nonviolent in word and deed. She reached out to the adversarial minority in her congregation, seeking to listen to their stories, many of which included painful relationships with gay and lesbian people in their families, and prayed with them. "My greatest prayer during that time was the ancient Jesus Prayer, 'Lord Jesus Christ, have mercy upon me, a sinner.' Every time I began to judge or distance myself from my adversaries, I cried out, 'God, have mercy upon me.' I knew that I couldn't preach and teach about acceptance if I was alienated from those whose viewpoints I opposed. The Jesus Prayer saved me from polarizing my church and destroying my ministry."

Stephanie's journey to prophetic hospitality was built upon the first-century vision of the body of Christ in which our individual joy and suffering, regardless of our role in the body, reflects and shapes the health of the whole. Her approach reflects the insight that God is present in every cell of Christ's body and that divine revelation can come from the most unlikely sources. Like many other prophetic pastors who take the time to pause, look, and listen, Stephanie discovered wisdom in those with whom she disagreed. She discovered that the people who opposed making an open and affirming statement "were not necessarily 'homophobic,' nor did they hate homosexuals. They simply had a different biblical starting point and life experience than the more liberal majority. They cherished Scripture and the traditions of the church and felt that we were turning away from our mission as Christians by taking an open and affirming stance."

In remembering to pray "God, have mercy," Stephanie, like many other spiritually centered pastors, made friends rather than enemies of those who opposed her theological and ethical viewpoints. Like many other pastors, Stephanie knew that she could not separate ends and means. She could not preach love if she disrespected her opponents. Through prayer and conversation involving people of all theological and ethical positions in her church, she was able to avoid polarization and unhelpful communication throughout the congregation's decision-making process. Ultimately, only a handful of people left the congregation over the decision to become open and affirming; and most of these have returned as a result of Stephanie's commitment to stay in communion with them, regardless of their viewpoints.

Prophetic hospitality is a patient process of appreciative reflection and practice aimed at widening the circle of love despite differences. When a pastor takes time to *pause, notice, open, yield and stretch,* and *respond* in spiritual awareness, she can respond from the perspective of God's wisdom, which joins justice with reconciliation, vision with affirmation. When we engage in this process, we pause a moment to notice feelings of defensiveness in ourselves and others, and open ourselves to noticing and appreciating God's presence in their lives. We take a moment to open ourselves to God's reconciling hospitality that embraces friend and foe alike. We allow our vision to become aligned with God's vision as a prelude to responding with hospitality as well as honesty.

Transforming Prophetic Anger

No one can accuse the biblical prophets of being theological, ethical, or political doormats. Indeed, the Scriptures suggest that the prophets were often angry and vindictive on God's behalf. Their "Thus saith the Lord" put fear in the hearts of unjust rulers and business people alike. Listen to the divine anger, described in Amos 5: "I hate, I despise your festivals, and I take no delight in your solemn assemblies. Even though you offer me your burnt offerings and grain offerings, I will not accept them; . . . Take away from me the noise of your songs; I will not hasten to the melody of your harps. But let justice roll down like waters, and righteousness like an ever-flowing stream" (Amos 5:21–24).

To be sure, injustice has a cost to rich and poor alike. In its most exalted forms, prophetic anger is grounded in God's— and the prophet's—love for the people. Divine anger in its purest and most constructive form is the other side of God's vision of shalom. This divine pathos,[11] to use the words of Rabbi Abraham Joshua Heschel, reflects God's suffering as a result of the infidelities and consequent suffering of God's people. God truly hears and empathizes with the cries of the oppressed and experiences the hopelessness of the vulnerable. God laments the fact that God's beloved people will experience the consequences of their own injustice and idolatry. Listen closely and you will experience God's pain rather than anger in Amos's words of warning: "The time is surely coming, says the Lord GOD, when I will send a famine on the land; not a famine of bread, or a thirst for water, but of hearing the words of [God]. They shall wander from sea to sea, and from north to east; they shall run to and fro, seeking the word of [God], but they shall not find it (Amos 8:11–12).

Centuries later, the One who overturned the moneychangers' tables in the Jerusalem temple also lamented the hardheartedness of the citizens of Jerusalem and proclaimed forgiveness to those who crucified him. Images of divine anger, when seen as reflecting God's opposition to life-destructive behaviors, can inspire us toward passionate responses to social and interpersonal evils. Still, the love of God and our love for congregants must be the primary focus of social transformation. Open to our own struggles as well as the struggles of our congregants, we learn to be pastors as well as prophets in our congregations.[12]

Many of today's pastors are angry at their congregations' failures to respond to the injustices of our time. Some lash out in sermons and in offhand remarks; others swallow their anger; still others seethe beneath the surface, creating by their ambient and unspoken anger a gulf between themselves and those to whom they are called to pastor. Anger is powerful energy; it can cure as well as kill. Today's pastors are called to transform anger into the energy of love, not only for those who are forgotten and oppressed but also for ethically oblivious congregants.

As a result of two specific questions posed to him by his spiritual director, David was able to transform his anger into prophetic creativity. In the spirit of Jesus's encounter with the man at the pool at Beth-zatha (John 5), David's spiritual director asked him, "Which pathway will you choose—the way of anger or the way of love? Which approach will best help you inspire your congregation to seek justice in your community— alienation or reconciliation?" After stuttering a few minutes in indignation at her pointed question, David had an epiphany in which he realized "How can I empower the members of my congregation to be more loving with the strangers in our community if I constantly judge and berate my congregants? I can't inspire them to love strangers if I don't love the people in my own faith community." At that "aha" moment David chose the path of prophetic hospitality and creativity. Although he still becomes impatient at times with the glacial changes he sees in his congregation, now he sees the people as God's beloved children, not political and social adversaries. David asserts, "When I made a commitment to see them through the eyes of Christ, amazing things happened—first to me and then in their lives. All of a sudden I communicated my social concerns more clearly and cooperatively and they returned the favor, even when they disagreed with me."

When he chose to see and, then, appreciate parishioners from a perspective other than judgment and alienation, David experienced the prophetic imagination. His church still struggles to be socially active, but now David recognizes that for his vision to be embodied, he must be willing to let his vision also be transformed by the many other positive, although less dramatic, visions of wholeness and shalom in the congregation. David began to experience God's presence and gentle movements toward spiritual transformation in his parishioners, and out of this new appreciative perspective, David found areas of common ground with people he had previously judged as reactionary or apathetic. While a transformed mind does not guarantee a transformed congregation and pastors may still have to place limits on exclusionary behaviors in their congregations, it calls us pastors to take responsibility for the only congregational reality we can truly change, our own mind and behavior.

Practicing Spirit-Centered Anger

While practicing the presence of God in prophetic ministry does not deny the positive value of anger as energy for transformation, it counsels us to channel our anger in ways that create rather destroy relationships and communities. First, healthy spirituality calls us to recognize, appreciate, and, then, let go of the anger we feel toward congregants, even if we feel that our anger is justified. In the words of Ephesians 4:26, "Be angry but do not sin; do not let the sun go down on your anger." It is clear that we must not deny our anger. Indeed anger, as the civil rights movement demonstrates, can be a force for good, when channeled in life-transforming and community-reconciling ways. But when we hold onto anger, allowing it to fester over time, we begin to see others' imperfections rather than God's presence in their lives. In contrast, spirit-centered approaches to anger appreciate and affirm the presence of God as the deepest reality of those with whom we contend.

Second, spirit-centered anger is grounded in the recognition that our perspective is always limited. *Apophatic* approaches to spirituality, grounded in the recognition that we can never fully fathom God and those around us, remind us that "we know only in part" and that "we see in a mirror, dimly" (1 Cor. 13:9, 12). Even our visions of justice are imperfect in light of God's reign of shalom. An apophatic approach to social transformation sees the truth as larger than any one perspective, including our own perspective, and listens for deeper revelations in conversation and in creative partnerships that may take us beyond our theological and ethical comfort zones.

Third, spirit-centered anger looks for the truth wherever it is found, even among our adversaries within the congregation. Following the *kataphatic* approach, grounded in the affirmation of God's universal presence, we look for God's wisdom in the many possible visions of justice within our congregation. The abundance of possible visions calls us to see the truth in our adversaries' positions and look for larger truth that embraces as many visions of truth and justice as possible. We can affirm our vision of justice flexibly as we await new and larger revelations of God's shalom.

Fourth, spirit-centered approaches to anger challenge us to cultivate what Mahatma Gandhi called *satyagraha*, or "soul force," by which our anger at those who perpetuate injustice is transformed into a passion for justice and reconciliation for all parties concerned. When we seek to embody soul force, we can explore our own tendencies toward violence, manifest in stereotyping, objectifying, ignoring, and demeaning our adversaries either in public behavior or private self-talk. Today in our polarized political environment, we need to model praying for political leaders whether or not we would consider voting for them.

Fifth, when we commit ourselves to see Christ in all of Christ's adversarial and distressing disguises, we learn to listen for God's presence in the words of others. As one central

Pennsylvania pastor noted, "I used to intellectually and emotionally shut down when my parishioners talked about their right to bear arms or their belief that opposing the war in Iraq was unpatriotic. I still don't agree with them and sometimes share my own opinions, but now I recognize that they are concerned about protecting their country and their families and have a vision of America that is important to them even though it's different from my own. Perhaps we can find something to talk about after all. They won't experience a larger vision of the gospel unless I am willing to listen as well as preach to them."

Sixth, practicing the presence of God in prophetic ministry challenges us to join daily prayerful examinations of conscience with theologically grounded social activism. We suggest that pastors regularly ask themselves questions such as the following:

1. In our quest for justice for the vulnerable and voice for the voiceless, do we turn away from those with whom we disagree?
2. In our quest to provide a home for all people, do we create spiritual homelessness among our congregants by not giving honor to the faithful service and love for the church of those who disagree with or resist our prophetic vision?
3. Are we affirming of diversity only to a certain point, but intolerant of people with whom we strongly disagree?
4. Do we listen patiently to people with whom we disagree, or do we tend to shut them down verbally and emotionally?
5. Further, do we demonize those with whom we disagree politically or political leaders whose values we perceive to be destructive of our nation and the planet?
6. Does our anger get in the way of healing our community and living by God's vision of shalom?

The practice of confession and examination of conscience does not call us to moral relativism or to acceptance of social and political injustice. The limitations of our own perspectives do not disqualify us from seeking to creatively transform our own lives and the world in which we live. In fact, recognizing our finitude and imperfection may inspire a greater passion for creative coalition building that leads to more effective social and political transformation.

Regular examinations of conscience remind us that we are all God's beloved children, each of whom is called to reflect God's grace and inspiration in her or his own unique way. When we cry out "God, have mercy upon me," we join the cries of creation's hope for wholeness, transformation, and shalom.

Practicing the Presence of God in Prophetic Ministry

In ministerial practice, prophetic ministry often divides more than it unites congregations. Nevertheless, faithful and spiritually centered ministry seeks reconciliation as an essential aspect of the prophetic challenge to persons, congregations, and institutions. Prophetic hospitality invites us to stay in relationship with those with whom we disagree through spiritual practices that enable us to pay attention to God's presence in the lives of our opponents as well as our supporters. While this is one of the most difficult tasks of ministry, seeing Christ in our adversaries enables us to focus on God's vision of shalom rather than our own more limited perspectives.

Discerning Your Prophetic Calling

God calls each person to be God's partner in healing the world. The nature of our prophetic calling differs according to our age, gifts, talents, life experiences, and, in the case of pastors, our congregational context. Our callings may lead us to social and political action in the spirit of Martin Luther King Jr., William Sloane Coffin Jr., Dorothy Day, and Desmond Tutu; or they may lead us to moment-by-moment random acts of kindness and tender mercy, especially toward vulnerable people and those whom we would describe as enemies in our particular congregation and community. In either case, as pastors we provide an alternative vision and alternative behaviors amid the alienation, violence, objectification, and hopelessness that characterize our time.

In this contemplative practice, which may last several weeks or even months, the two of us invite you to regularly take time amid the daily activities of ministry for silent listening and meditation focused on Isaiah's vision of God in the temple (Isa. 6:1–8). Take time to reflect on Isaiah's sense of sinfulness, "Woe is me . . . for I am a [sinful person]," and God's word to the prophet, "Whom shall I send?" In the silence, consider the circles of relationship that characterize your ministry. Visualize the members of your congregation, groups within your congregation, the larger community, people in need in the community, the nation, and the planet. Visualize vulnerable, neglected, and marginalized people living in your community. Do you feel an affinity with any particular group? Ask and listen for God's response to your call: Where will you send me, God? What is right for my time and energy, and my passion, in this time? What is right for my congregation at this time?

No doubt, you may hear many voices and see many faces within your congregation and community that reflect God's call. Let these faces and voices inspire further questions. While our community has many needs to which we are called to respond, we as pastors can, practically speaking, only follow one significant prophetic vision at a time.

As you gain discernment for your particular prophetic calling for this time and place, take time to share it with key people in your congregation. Invite them to pray with you and help you listen for God's voice in the many needs of your community and where you and they might respond. You may choose to form a spirituality and social concerns group whose goal is to respond with prayer and sensitivity as well as with a sense of your congregation's gifts and limitations.

Safe in God's Care

Prophetic hospitality will always be met with resistance from people within our congregations. Whether such resistance comes from others' heartfelt theological positions or their love of a long-standing congregational identity that they perceive is threatened by your prophetic innovations, it can raise a pastor's level of fear and anxiety at a time when it is especially important that she remain a nonanxious presence.[13] The two of us believe that the practices we have mentioned in this book contribute to the sense of peace, reconciliation, and perspective needed for nonanxious leadership, whether you seek to transform congregational culture or to inspire commitment to social justice. To be sure, prayerful contemplation, devotional reading, and self-care help nurture a peaceful center in the midst of the storms of prophetic ministry. Further, affirmative and appreciative reflection enables us to experience God's presence in challenging people and situations. Practicing the presence of God throughout one's ministry enables a prophetically hospitable pastor to respond from a quiet spiritual center in conflict situations rather than with anxiety, anger, and alienation.

We suggest one more practice that can deepen your sense of God's presence and protection when you are facing resistance as a result of your quest for justice: the Celtic spiritual practice of encircling, or *caim*. When you begin a journey, encounter adversity, or face conflict, simply inscribe a circle around yourself in a clockwise fashion with your index finger. As you draw a circle, imagine yourself safe and protected in God's care in every situation. Within God's unbroken circle, you are safe and strong, peaceful and calm.

In the midst of a contentious meeting, you can take a moment and visualize this circle, first encompassing you and then everyone in the group. You may also choose to say the prayer of St. Patrick, which describes Christ as being above, beneath, and on every side, or invoke a prayer such as, "I place myself in your protection, O God," or "Let your peace surround me."

Seeing Christ in Adversaries

In this spiritual exercise, begin with silent listening and breathing, inhaling deeply the caring presence of God. After spending several minutes in quiet and prayerful breathing, as you exhale begin to visualize the many circles of relationship in your ministry—personal, congregational, denominational, local, national, and planetary. Visualize the many different people involved in your ministerial care.

Now take a few moments to consider those people whom you see as political and congregational adversaries. Visualize them face by face, first noticing the feelings that your visualization then brings up. Note your past and current feelings toward them as you recall your disagreement or conflict with them. Then, in the spirit of appreciative and affirmative reflection, make an effort to ponder the truths within their perspectives and the gifts they bring to the conversation. Visualize them as surrounded by God's healing and loving light. Despite your differences, experience yourself as joined in spirit with them by visualizing the two of you connected and surrounded by God's light.

As you conclude, take a few minutes to pray for God's guidance in living out your beliefs and newly gained appreciation and in recognizing your limitations. Take a few moments to ask God to guide your adversaries, along with yourself, as partners in creative transformation toward God's dream of shalom.

CONCLUSION

Awakening to God's Presence in Ministry

Rejoice in [God] always; again, I will say, Rejoice. Let your gentleness be known to everyone. [God] is near. Do not worry about anything, but in everything by prayer and supplication with thanksgiving let your requests be made known to God. And the peace of God, which surpasses all understanding, will guard your hearts and minds in Christ Jesus.

—PHILIPPIANS 4:4–7

These words to the faithful followers of Jesus at Philippi describe what it means for pastors and laypeople to practice the presence of God in their respective ministries. Throughout this book, we have noted the importance of vision, promise, and practice in faithful, spirit-centered, and effective ministry. Our beliefs and affirmations truly do matter. They shape our responses to ordinary as well as unexpected events in ministry. Our beliefs provide the lenses through which we see God's presence in everyday life and in moments of crisis. The theological center of this text is the affirmation that God is present in every moment of our lives, intimately seeking wholeness, beauty, and justice. We can experience God because God is near (Phil. 4:5) to each one of us, and is indeed the dynamic and personal reality in whom "we live and move and have our being" (Acts 17:28). God gracefully calls us to wholeness in every moment and encounter.

From this vision of God's intimate and inspiring presence comes a great promise, articulated in many ways throughout Scripture and human experience. Jesuit spiritual guide Jean-Pierre de Caussade described this promise as the "sacrament of the present moment."[1] The Quakers proclaim the inner light present in all people, despite the differences of race, gender, sexual identity, nation, or economics. Described as the "light of all people" (John 1:4), Jesus challenged his followers to see themselves as the light of the world, whose shining brings glory to God. In this book, we celebrate Brother Lawrence's counsel to practice the presence of God every moment of our lives.

We believe that the promise of God's presence is at the heart of faithful, creative, healthy, and life-transforming ministry. God is present, inspiring, challenging, and comforting us in each moment of pastoral ministry. Each of the routine and necessary tasks of ministry—preaching, worship leadership, teaching, spiritual direction, pastoral care, leadership and administration, and prophetic hospitality—can be a window through which we and our congregants experience God's lively, transforming presence.

The vision and promise of God's constant presence inspire spiritual practices that can transform our lives and ministry. Paul captures the essence of practicing the presence of God in congregational life with these words addressed to the Philippian community: "Finally, beloved, whatever is true, whatever is honorable, whatever is just, whatever is pure, whatever is pleasing, whatever is commendable, if there is any excellence and if there is anything worthy of praise, think about these things. Keep on doing the things that you have learned and received and heard and seen in me, and the God of peace will be with you" (Phil. 4:8–9).

Grace abounds in your ministry and in your daily life. It may come unexpectedly along the Damascus road or through an angelic visit. But, most of the time, we need to "think about these things," that is, to tend the holy by cultivating daily practices of God's presence in our personal and professional lives. While the two of us affirm a multiplicity of spiritual practices related to a variety of factors, including age, gender, personality type, life experience, ethnicity, and religious background, we assert that these many practices of faith reflect our commitment to *pause, notice, open, yield and stretch,* and then *respond* to God's lively grace in our lives.

Although there is no *one* pathway to practicing the presence of God in ministry, we encourage you to explore simple everyday practices that can be reminders of God's presence in any situation, as well as more complex practices, such as centering prayer, visualization exercises, and spiritual retreats, that require dedicated times throughout the day, week, or year. Everyday practices, such as breath prayers and the Jesus Prayer, open us to experience God's inspiring presence moment by moment, whether in a hospital room or church board meeting.

As we look at ministry today, the two of us are hopeful that pastors can experience God's grace in every moment of ministry. Our hope is grounded in God's graceful and abundant presence that is sufficient for every pastoral situation. We can practice God's presence faithfully because God is here with us right now, and "God will fully satisfy every need of yours according to [God's] riches in glory in Christ Jesus" (Phil. 4:19). As pastors, we can "do all things"—we can balance innovative and faithful ministry with personal and relational well-being—through God "who strengthens" us (Phil. 4:13), by opening to a grace and energy that is always more than we can imagine as we practice the presence of God in ministry.

Notes

FOREWORD

1. See World Union Shabbat Evening Services published by the World Union for Progressive Judaism online at http://wupj.org/Assets/Brochures/ShabbatService.pdf. Also quoted in Rachel Naomi Remen, *My Grandfather's Blessings: Stories of Strength, Refuge, and Belonging* (New York: Riverhead Books, 2000).

2. Kent Ira Groff, *The Soul of Tomorrow's Church: Weaving Spiritual Practices in Ministry Together* (Nashville: Upper Room Books, 2000). See especially chapter 5, "The Soul of Education."

3. Clarissa Pinkola Estes, *Women Who Run with the Wolves: Myths and Stories of the Wild Woman Archetype* (New York: Ballantine Books, 1992), 464.

INTRODUCTION

1. We have chosen, with rare exceptions, to change names, denominations, and sometimes locations to preserve the privacy of our pastoral conversations. In a few cases, we have created composites that mirror the experiences of a number of pastors who have shared their journeys with us.

2. Diana Butler Bass, *The Practicing Congregation: Imagining a New Old Church* (Herndon, VA: Alban Institute, 2004) and

Christianity for the Rest of Us: How the Neighborhood Church Is Transforming the Faith (San Francisco: HarperOne, 2006).

3. Dorothy Bass, ed., *Practicing Our Faith: A Way of Life for a Searching People* (San Francisco: Jossey-Bass, 1999), 5.

4. Brother Lawrence, *The Practice of the Presence of God* (New Kensington, PA: Whitaker House, 1982), 61.

5. Ibid., 62.

6. Jean-Pierre de Caussade, *The Sacrament of the Present Moment* (New York: HarperSanFrancisco, 1989), 1.

7. Ibid., 2.

8. Norvene Vest, *Preferring Christ: A Devotional Commentary and Workbook on the Rule of St. Benedict* (Harrisburg, PA: Morehouse, 2004), 1.

9. *Feed the Fire! Avoiding Clergy Burnout* (Cleveland: Pilgrim Press, 2008) and *Four Seasons of Ministry: Gathering a Harvest of Righteousness* (Herndon, VA: Alban Institute, 2008).

10. The initialism *INFJ* (Introvert-Intuitive-Feeling-Judging) relates to one of the personality constellations identified by Carl Jung, which Isabel Myers and Katherine Briggs developed into an assessment tool, the Myers-Briggs Type Indicator. For more on Jungian personality types as these relate to ministry, we refer you to Bruce Epperly, *Feed the Fire! Avoiding Clergy Burnout*, 139–58. An INFJ tends to find his or her energy in times of reflection, meets the world through her or his feelings, makes decisions based on context and overall responsiveness to situations, and generally seeks a life that is orderly while open to novelty.

11. An ENFP (Extrovert-Intuitive-Feeling-Perceiving) shares many of the same characteristics as an INFJ (the NF), but finds energy in external relationships and encounters the world in the moment rather than by a definite plan.

12. Joyce Rupp, *The Cup of Our Life: A Guide for Spiritual Growth* (Notre Dame, IN: Ave Maria Press, 1997).

13. For more on the vision of divine-human creativity, see Bruce Epperly, *Holy Adventure: 41 Days of Audacious Living* (Nashville: Upper Room, 2008).

14. Kathleen Norris, *The Quotidian Mysteries: Laundry, Liturgy, and "Women's Work"* (New York: Paulist Press, 1998), 63.

15. For an inspirational summary of Thich Nhat Hanh, we suggest *Peace Is Every Step: The Path of Mindfulness in Everyday Life* (New York: Bantam Books, 1991).

16. Gerald May, *The Awakened Heart: Opening Yourself to the Love You Need* (San Francisco: HarperSanFrancisco, 1991), 115–20. While forms of this practice appear throughout May's book, this is the most concise statement.

17. Ibid., 111.

18. Ibid., 54.

19. Ibid., 117.

CHAPTER 1

1. Marilynne Robinson, *Gilead* (New York: Farrar, Strauss and Giroux, 2004), 232.

2. Mike Graves, *The Fully Alive Preacher: Recovering from Homiletical Burnout* (Louisville: Westminster John Knox, 2006), 3.

3. Charles Wesley, 1707–1788, "Love Divine, All Loves Excelling."

4. Marcus Borg , *Meeting Jesus Again for the First Time* (New York: Harper One, 1995), 32–33.

5. The purpose of the Center for Process Studies is to integrate the insights of process theology with everyday life. For more on the Process and Faith Lectionary Commentary, see www.processandfaith.org.

6. Karl Barth, *Church Dogmatics*, vol. 3, *The Doctrine of Creation*, pt. 4, eds. G. F. Bromily and T. F. Torrance (Edinburgh: T & T Clark, 1969), 68. Cited in Mike Graves's book, *The Fully Alive Preacher*.

7. Frederick Buechner, *Listening to Your Life* (New York: Harper One, 1992), and Parker Palmer, *Let Your Life Speak: Listening for the Voice of Vocation* (San Francisco: Jossey-Bass, 1999).

8. Edward P. Wimberly, *Recalling Our Stories: Spiritual Renewal for Religious Caregivers* (San Francisco: Jossey-Bass, 1997).

9. For more on God's call throughout a pastor's lifetime, see Bruce Epperly and Katherine Epperly, *The Four Seasons of Ministry: Gathering a Harvest of Righteousness* (Herndon, VA: Alban Institute, 2008).

10. Barbara S. Blaisdell, "Mother to Mother: Centered in a Circle of Need," in *Birthing the Sermon: Women Preachers on the Creative Process*, ed. Jana Childers, 1–14 (St. Louis: Chalice, 2001), 5.

11. Jack Good, *The Dishonest Church* (Bend, OR: Rising Star Press, 2003), 12.

12. Linda L. Clader, "Homily for the Feast of Visitation," in *Birthing the Sermon*, 51–66 (see note 10), 56.

13. Ibid., 57.

14. Ibid., 12.

15. Ibid., 39.

16. Alfred North Whitehead, *Process and Reality*, corr. ed. (New York: Free Press, 1978), 102.

17. Graves, *The Fully Alive Preacher*, 82.

18. James F. White, *Introduction to Christian Worship* (Nashville: Abingdon, 2000), 23.

19. Gordon Lathrop, *Holy Ground: A Liturgical Cosmology* (Minneapolis: Fortress Press, 2003), 5.

20. Julian of Norwich, *Showings*, trans. Edmund Colledge, O.S.B., and James Walsh, S.J. (New York: Paulist Press, 1978), 183.

21. Annie Dillard, *Pilgrim at Tinker Creek* (New York: Harper's Magazine Press, 1974), 14–15.

22. Texts in the area of emerging worship include Jonny Baker, *Alternative Worship: Resources from and for the Emerging*

Church (London: Society for Promoting Christian Knowledge, 2003); John L. Bell, *The Singing Thing: A Case for Congregational Song* (Chicago: GIA, 2000); Robert Webber, *Ancient-Future Worship: Proclaiming and Enacting God's Narrative* (Grand Rapids: Baker Books, 2008).

23. Abraham Joshua Heschel, *Man Is Not Alone: A Philosophy of Religion* (New York: Farrar, Straus, and Giroux, 1976), 13.

24. Al Carmines, "Many Gifts, One Spirit" (also known as "God of Change and Glory"). Used by permission.

25. Kent Ira Groff, *What Would I Believe If I Didn't Believe Anything? A Handbook for Spiritual Orphans* (San Francisco: Jossey-Bass, 2004).

26. Anne Lamott, *Plan B: Further Thoughts on Faith* (New York: Riverhead Books, 2005), 295.

27. David L. Fleming, *The Spiritual Exercises of St. Ignatius: A Literal Translation and a Contemporary Reading* (St. Louis: Institute of Jesuit Sources, 1978).

28. Archie Matson, *A Month with the Master: A Devotional Manual Based on the Ignatian Method of Spiritual Exercises* (n.p.: Disciplined Order of Christ, 1958).

CHAPTER 2

1. Groff, *What Would I Believe*.

2. Martin Luther King Jr., "Letter from Birmingham City Jail" (Philadelphia: American Friends Service Committee, May 1963), 12.

3. Borg, *Meeting Jesus Again*, 32–33.

4. See Gerald May, *The Dark Night of the Soul: A Psychiatrist Explores the Connection between Darkness and Spiritual Growth* (New York: Harper One, 2005) and Renita Weems, *Listening for God: A Minister's Journey Through Silence and Doubt* (New York: Simon and Schuster, 1999).

5. Eugene Peterson, *Working the Angles: The Shape of Pastoral Integrity* (Grand Rapids: Eerdmanns, 1987).

6. Kenneth Leach, *Soul Friend: A Study of Spirituality* (London: Sheldon Press, 1977), 69.

7. Tilden Edwards, *Spiritual Director, Spiritual Companion: Guide to Tending the Soul* (New York: Paulist Press, 2001), 23–24.

8. Gerald May, *Care of Mind, Care of Spirit: The Psychiatric Dimensions of Spiritual Direction* (San Francisco: Harper Row, 1982), 6.

9. *The Way of the Pilgrim and The Pilgrim Continues His Way*, translated by R. M. French (New York: HarperSanFrancisco, 1965).

10. Thich Nhat Hanh, *Peace Is Every Step*, 10.

11. Bruce G. Epperly and Katherine Gould Epperly, *The Four Seasons of Ministry: A Harvest of Righteousness* (Herndon, VA: The Alban Institute, 2008), 42.

12. For more on spiritual attunements in medicine and ministry see Candace Pert, *Molecules of Emotion: The Science Behind Mind-Body Medicine* (New York: Simon and Schuster, 1999); Bruce Epperly, *God's Touch: Faith, Wholeness, and the Healing Miracles of Jesus* (Louisville: Westminster John Knox, 2001); Stephanie Mines, "Whose Hand is This? Attunement and Bodywork," *Massage and Bodywork*, January/February 2009, 45–46, 49–55.

13. Edwards, *Spiritual Director, Spiritual Companion*, 23.

14. Margaret Guenther, *Holy Listening: The Art of Spiritual Direction* (Cambridge, MA: Cowley Publications, 1992), 11.

15. Thomas Merton, *The Wisdom of the Desert: Sayings from the Desert Fathers of the Fourth Century* (New York: New Directions, 1970), 47.

16. John Yungblut, *The Gentle Art of Spiritual Guidance* (Rockport, MA: Element Books, 1988).

17. May, *Care of Mind, Care of Spirit*, 95.

18. Ibid., 15.

19. De Cassaude, *Sacrament of the Present Moment* (New York: HarperSanFrancisco, 1989).

20. Thich Nhat Hanh, *Living Buddha, Living Christ* (New York: Riverhead Books, 1995), 23.

21. George Fox, quoted in Yungblut, *Gentle Art of Spiritual Guidance*, 55.

CHAPTER 3

1. For more on the healings of Jesus, see Bruce Epperly, *God's Touch: Faith, Wholeness, and the Healing Miracles of Jesus* (Louisville: Westminster John Knox, 2001).

2. Walter Brueggemann, *Spirituality of the Psalms* (Minneapolis: Fortress Press, 2001), 8–11.

3. Alan Jones, preface to Guenther, *Holy Listening*, x.

4. Gordon E. Jackson, *Pastoral Care and Process Theology* (Lanham, MD: University Press of America, 1981), 52.

5. Edward P. Wimberly, *Claiming God, Reclaiming Dignity: African American Pastoral Care* (Nashville: Abingdon, 2003), 51.

6. Bernard Loomer, "S-I-Z-E is the Measure," in *Religious Experience and Process Theology: The Pastoral Implications of a Major Modern Movement*, eds. Harry James Cargas and Bernard Lee (New York: Paulist Press, 1976), 70.

7. Edwin H. Friedman, *Generation to Generation: Family Process in Church and Synagogue* (New York: Guilford, 1985); and Peter L. Steinke, *Congregational Leadership in Anxious Times: Being Calm and Courageous No Matter What* (Herndon, VA: Alban Institute, 2006).

8. Peggy Way, *Created by God: Pastoral Care for All God's People* (St. Louis: Chalice Press, 2005), 17.

9. Parker Palmer, *A Hidden Wholeness: The Journey Toward an Undivided Life* (San Francisco: Jossey-Bass, 2004).

10. Henri J. M. Nouwen, *The Wounded Healer: Ministry in Contemporary Society* (New York: Image Books, 1979).

11. Tara Brach, *Radical Acceptance: Embracing Your Life with the Heart of a Buddha* (New York: Bantam Books, 2003), 4, 25,

26. We are grateful to Melinda Reed and Cyndi Simpson for recommending Brach's work to us.

12. LGBTQ is an acronym for those people who identify themselves as lesbian, gay, bisexual, transgendered, and questioning regarding their sexual identity.

13. Linda J. Schupp, *Assessing and Treating Trauma and PTSD* (Eau Claire, WI: Pesi, 2004), 107 (our italics).

14. For more on Jesus's healing ministry, see Bruce Epperly, *God's Touch* and *Healing Worship: Purpose and Practice* (Cleveland: Pilgrim Press, 2006).

15. Rita Nakashima Brock and Rebecca Ann Parker, *Proverbs of Ashes: Violence, Redemptive Suffering, and the Search for What Saves Us* (Boston: Beacon Press, 2001), 20–22.

16. Brach, *Radical Acceptance*, 243–45.

CHAPTER 4

1. For an illuminating discussion on the spiritual and pastoral dimensions of administration and management, see Louis B. Weeks, *All for God's Glory: Redeeming Church Scutwork* (Herndon, VA: Alban Institute, 2008).

2. Mark Lau Branson, *Memories, Hopes, and Conversations: Appreciative Inquiry and Congregational Change* (Herndon, VA: Alban Institute, 2004), 27.

3. Whitehead, *Process and Reality*, 244.

4. For more on appreciative inquiry, see David L. Cooperrider and Diana Kaplin Whitney, *Appreciative Inquiry: A Positive Revolution in Change* (San Francisco: Barrett-Koehler, 2005); Branson, *Memories, Hopes, and Conversations*; Robert J. Voyle and Kim M. Voyle, *Core Elements of the Appreciative Way: An Introduction to Appreciative Inquiry for Work and Daily Living* (Hillsboro, OR: Clergy Leadership Institute, 2006).

5. Dag Hammarskjold, *Markings* (New York: Vintage, 1989), 89.

6. John Heider, *The Tao of Leadership: Lao Tzu's Tao Te Ching Adapted for a New Age* (Atlanta: Humanics, 1997), 3.

7. Bernard Loomer, "Two Conceptions of Power," *Process Studies* 6, no. 1 (Spring 1976): 8.

8. Ibid., 18.

9. G. Lloyd Rediger, *Clergy Killers: Guidance for Pastors and Congregations Under Attack* (Louisville: Westminster John Knox, 1997).

10. Quoted in Lovett Weems, *Church Leadership: Vision, Team, Culture, and Integrity* (Nashville: Abingdon, 1993), 53.

11. Gerald G. Jampolsky, *Love Is Letting Go of Fear* (Milbrae, CA: Celestial Arts, 1979) and *Goodbye to Guilt: Releasing Fear through Forgiveness* (New York: Bantam Books, 1985); Susan Trout, *To See Differently: Personal Growth and Being of Service through Attitudinal Healing* (Washington, DC: Three Roses Press, 1990).

12. For more on the use of spiritual affirmations, see Bruce Epperly, *Holy Adventure*, and *The Power of Affirmative Faith* (St. Louis: Chalice, 2001).

13. We are especially indebted to the work of David Cooperrider in creating appreciative inquiry as a tool for transformation. In this section, we have elaborated on the appreciative inquiry process found in David Cooperrider and Diana Whitney's book *Appreciative Inquiry*.

CHAPTER 5

1. Matthew 25:31–46 asserts that our relationship with God is intimately connected with our care for the most vulnerable of God's children. We love God in our relationships with the most disadvantaged members of our community, according to Jesus: "As you did it to one of the least of these who are members of my family, you did it to me" (v. 40).

2. Marcus Borg and N. T. Wright, *The Meaning of Jesus: Two Visions* (New York: Harper Collins, 1999), 33, 38.

3. Ibid., 70.

4. John Dominic Crossan, *Jesus: A Revolutionary Biography* (San Francisco: HarperSanFrancisco, 1994), 64, 55.

5. Walter Brueggemann, *The Prophetic Imagination* (Minneapolis: Fortress Press, 2001), ix, xx.

6. Delia Halverson, *The Gift of Hospitality: In Church, in the Home, in All of Life* (St. Louis: Chalice Press, 1999), 13, 16.

7. Amy Oden, *God's Welcome: Hospitality for a Gospel-Hungry World* (Cleveland: Pilgrim Press, 2008), 14, 7.

8. Ibid., 63.

9. Halverson, *Gift of Hospitality*, 37.

10. For more on Silent Witness, see www.silentwitnesspa.org.

11. Abraham Joshua Heschel, *Between God and Man: An Interpretation of Judaism from the Writings of Abraham Joshua Heschel* (New York: Harper and Row, 1959), 123–24.

12. We are grateful to Julia O'Brien's insights in *Challenging Prophetic Metaphor: Theology and Ideology in the Prophets* (Louisville: Westminster John Knox, 2008) that serve as a reminder that many of these prophetic passages are profoundly ambiguous—they speak of social transformation in words that are violent, oppressive, and misogynist.

13. For the spirituality of becoming a nonanxious presence, we refer you to Bruce and Katherine Epperly, *Feed the Fire*, 121–38.

CONCLUSION

1. De Caussade, *Sacrament of the Present Moment*.